Frederick the Great on Warfare

Frederick the Great on Warfare

Battlefield Tactics of the Seven Year's War

Military Instruction to the Officers of His Army,

Frederick II, King of Prussia
Translated from the French
By Thomas Foster

LEONAUR

Frederick the Great on Warfare
Battlefield Tactics of the Seven Year's War
Military Instruction to the Officers of His Army
by Frederick II, King of Prussia
Translated from the French by Thomas Foster

First published under the title
Military Instruction from the Late King of Prussia to His Generals and
Particular Instruction to the Officers of His Army, and Especially Those of the Cavalry

Leonaur is an imprint of Oakpast Ltd

ISBN: 978-1-78282-559-3 (hardcover)
ISBN: 978-1-78282-560-9 (softcover)

http://www.leonaur.com

Publisher's Notes

The views expressed in this book are not necessarily
those of the publisher.

Contents

To Major-General Goldsworthy,
First Equerry to His Majesty,
Colonel of the First (or Royal) Regiment of Dragoons,
&c., &c., &c.

Sir,

It is to your kindness that I owe my introduction to a profession whose useful and honourable practice the following sheets are intended to illustrate and improve.

The same disposition inclined you to commend my present humble undertaking, and to sanction it with the honour of your name.

Such indulgence affords me the highest gratification, as it gives support to my weak endeavours, justifies the proud boast of holding some place in your friendship, and gives an opportunity to declare with how much real respect and gratitude

I am, Sir,

Your very obliged, obedient Servant,

T. Foster.

Wells, Somerset, March, 1797.

Preface to the First Edition

The translation of the first of the following treatises was undertaken from the circumstance of not being able to procure a copy of that publication, which about thirty years ago made its appearance in the world. I have, however, since my design has been carried into execution, obtained a sight of it from a military friend, and have only to add, that if the translator of that day be still alive, the contrast between the two publications will have the effect of flattering his *amour propre*, instead of awakening his jealousy.

The latter treatise, as far as my own enquiries and those of my friends can discover, was never exhibited in an English dress till it appeared in that plain garb which it received from me during the last summer.

As private information and public utility were the real motives of each undertaking, simplicity and perspicuity of language have been the chief objects of attention; roundness of period and elegance of diction (had they been in my power) would have embellished the work, but not improved it.

It is not pretended (for my slender acquaintance with the language forbade such exactness) that every phrase is construed in perfect conformity to the French idiom; in some cases, perhaps, so close a translation would be impracticable; in others less difficult, ignorance (I hope not inattention) may have occasioned some deviation from the true meaning, though I presume in no glaring or important degree.

On the utility of either work, I need say nothing, for where so properly can a British officer look for information, as in the rudiments of that school which had the honour to lay the foundation of the military education of our royal and illustrious commander in chief?

I feel much indebted to those officers who have honoured me with their countenance, and particularly those whose rank and reputation in the service have not kept them back from favouring an undertaking which can offer nothing new to minds so enlightened and informed.

T. Foster

Military Instruction from the Late King of Prussia to His Generals

The First Treatise

Of Prussian Troops, their Excellencies and their Defects

The strictest care and the most unremitting attention are required of commanding officers in the formation of my troops. The most exact discipline is ever to be maintained, and the greatest regard paid to their welfare; they ought also to be better fed than almost any troops in Europe.

Our regiments are composed of half our own people and half foreigners who enlist for money: the latter only wait for a favourable opportunity to quit a service to which they have no particular attachment. The prevention of desertion therefore becomes an object of importance.

Many of our generals regard one man as good in effect as another, and imagine that if the vacancy be filled up, this man has no influence on the whole; but one does not know how on this subject to make a proper application of other armies to our own.

If a deserter be replaced by a man as well trained and disciplined as himself, it is a matter of no consequence; but if a soldier, who for two years has been accustomed to arms and military exercise, should desert, and be replaced by a bad subject, or perhaps none at all, the consequence must prove eventually very material.

It has happened from the negligence of officers in this particular; that regiments have not only been lessened in number, but that they have also lost their reputation.

By accidents of this kind, the army becomes weakened at the very period when its completion is most essentially necessary, and unless the greatest attention be paid to this circumstance, you will lose the best of your forces and never be able to recover yourself.

Though my country be well peopled, it is doubtful if many men are to be met with of the height of my soldiers: and supposing even that there was no want of them, could they be disciplined in an instant? It therefore becomes one of the most essential duties of generals who command armies or detachments, to prevent desertion. This is to be effected,

1st. By not encamping too near a wood or forest, unless sufficient reason require it.

2ndly. By calling the roll frequently every day.

3rdly. By often sending out patrols of hussars, to scour the country round about the camp.

4thly. By placing *chasseurs* in the corn by night, and doubling the cavalry posts at dusk to strengthen the chain.

5thly. By not allowing the soldiers to wander about and taking care that each troop be led regularly to water and forage by an officer.

6thly. By punishing all marauding with severity, as it gives rise to every species of disorder and irregularity.

7thly. By not drawing in the guards, who are placed in the villages on marching days, until the troops are under arms.

8thly. By forbidding, under the strictest injunctions, that any soldier on a march quit his rank or his division.

9thly. By avoiding night-marches, unless obliged by necessity.

10thly. By pushing forward patrols of hussars to the right and left, whilst the infantry are passing through a. wood.

11thly. By placing officers at each end of a defile, to oblige the soldiers to fall into their proper places.

12thly. By concealing from the soldier any retrograde movement which you may be obliged to make, or giving some specious flattering pretext for so doing.

13thly. By paying great attention to the regular issue of necessary subsistence and taking care that the troops be furnished with bread, flesh, beer, brandy, &c.

14thly. By searching for the cause of the evil, when desertion shall have crept into a regiment or company: enquiring if the soldier has received his bounty and other customary indulgencies, and if there has been no misconduct on the part of the captain. No relaxation of discipline is however on any account to be permitted. It may be said, that the colonel will take care of this business, but his efforts alone cannot be sufficient; for in an army, every individual part of it should aim at perfection, to make it appear to be the work of only one man.

An army is composed for the most part of idle and inactive men, and unless the general has a constant eye upon them, and obliges them to do their duty, this artificial machine, which with greatest care cannot be made perfect, will very soon fall to pieces, and nothing but the *bare idea* of a *disciplined army* will remain.

Constant employment for the troops is therefore indispensably necessary: the experience of officers who adopt such plan will convince them of its good effects, and they will also perceive that there are *daily* abuses to be corrected, which pass unobserved by those who are too indolent to endeavour to discover them.

This constant and painful attention may appear at first sight as rather a hardship on the general, but its consequences will make him ample amends. With troops so fine, so brave, and so well disciplined, what advantage can he not obtain? A general, who with other nations would be regarded as being rash or half mad, would with us be only acting by established rules. Any enterprise which man is capable of executing, may be undertaken by him. Besides this, the soldiers will not suffer a man to remain amongst them who has betrayed any symptoms of shyness, which would certainly not be regarded in other armies.

I have been an eye-witness to the conduct both of officers and private soldiers, who could not be prevailed on, though dangerously wounded, to quit their post, or fall into the rear to get themselves dressed. With troops like these the *world itself* might be subdued, if conquests were not as fatal to the victors as to the vanquished. Let them be but well supplied with provisions, and you may attempt anything with them. On a march you prevent the enemy by speed; at an attack of a wood, you will force them; if you make them climb a mountain, you will soon disperse those who make any resistance, and it then becomes an absolute massacre. If you put your cavalry into action, they will charge through the enemy at the sword's point and demolish them.

But as it is not alone sufficient that *the troops* be good, and as the ignorance of a *general* may be the means of losing every advantage, I shall proceed to speak of the qualities which a general ought to possess, and lay down such rules as I have either learned from well-informed generals, or purchased dearly by my own experience.

ARTICLE 2

Of the Subsistence of Troops, and of Provisions

It has been said by a certain general, that the first object in the establishment of an army ought to be making provision for the belly, that being the basis and foundation of all operations. I shall divide this subject into two parts: in the first I shall explain *how* and *where* magazines ought to be established, and in the latter, the method of *employing*, and of *transporting* them.

The first rule is to establish the large magazines invariably in the rear of the army, and, if possible, in a place that is well secured. During the wars in Silesia and Bohemia, our grand magazine was at Breslau, on account of the advantage of being able to replenish it by means of the Oder. When magazines are formed at the head of an army, the first check may oblige you to abandon them, and you may be left without resource: whereas, if they are established in the rear of each other, the war will be prudently carried on, and one small disaster will not complete your ruin.

Spandau and Magdebourg should be the chosen situations for magazines in the frontier of the Electorate. Magdebourg, on account of the Elbe, will be particularly serviceable in an offensive war against Saxony, and Schweidnitz against Bohemia.

You cannot be too cautious in the choice of commissaries and their deputies, for if they prove dishonest, the state will be materially injured. With this view, men of strict honour should be appointed as superiors, who must *personally*, *frequently*, and *minutely* examine and control the accounts.

There are two ways of forming magazines, either by ordering the nobility and peasants to bring their grain to the depot, and paying them for it according to the rate laid down by the chamber of finance, or by taking a certain quantity from them by requisition. It is the business of the commissary to settle and to sign all these agreements.

Vessels of a particular construction are built for the purpose of conveying corn and forage along the canals and rivers.

Purveyors are never to be employed but in cases of the last necessity, for even Jews are less exorbitant in their demands: they increase the price of provisions, and sell them out again at a most extravagant profit.

The magazines should be established at a very early period, that no

16

kind of necessary may be wanting when the army leaves its quarters to begin a campaign: if they be too long neglected, the frost will put a stop to water-carriage, or the roads will become so excessively deep and heavy, that their formation will be a business of the utmost difficulty.

Besides the regimental covered waggons which carry bread for eight days, the commissary is provided with conveniencies for carrying provisions for a month.

The advantage of *navigation* is, however, never to be neglected, for without this convenience, no army can ever be *abundantly* supplied.

The waggons should be drawn by horses; trial has been made of oxen, but they do not answer the purpose.

The waggon-masters must be exceedingly careful that due attention be paid to their cattle. The general of an army must have an eye to this circumstance, for the loss of horses will necessarily occasion a diminution of waggons, and consequently of provisions.

Moreover, unless they receive a proper quantity of good food, these horses will be unable to undergo the necessary fatigue. On a march, therefore, not only the horses will be lost, but also the waggons and their contents. The best concerted measures may be ruined by a repetition of such disasters. The general, therefore, must not neglect any of these circumstances, which are so materially important in all his operations.

In order to facilitate the carriage of provisions in a war against Saxony, advantage must be taken of the Elbe, and in Silesia of the Oder. The *sea* affords you this assignee in Prussia, but in Bohemia and Moravia, your only dependence is on *carriages*. It sometimes happens, that three or four depots of provisions are formed on the same line, as was the case with us in Bohemia in the year 1742. There was a magazine at Pardubitz, at Nienbourg, at Podjebrod, and at Brandies, to enable us to keep pace with the enemy, and follow him to Prague, if he had thought proper to have gone thither.

During the last campaign in Bohemia, Breslau furnished Schweidnitz, Schweidnitz supplied Jaromirez, and from thence provisions were carried to the army.

Besides the covered waggons which carry provisions, iron ovens always travel with the army, (the number of which has of late been very much augmented), and, on every halting day they are set to bake bread. On all expeditions, you should be supplied with bread or biscuit for ten days. Biscuit is a very good article, but our soldiers like it only in soup, nor do they know how to employ it to the best advantage.

On a march through an enemy's county, the depot of meal should ever be in a garrisoned town near the army. During the campaign of 1745, our depot was first at Neustadt, then at Jaromirez, and last at Trautenau. Had we been farther advanced, we could not have had a depot in security nearer than that at Pardubitz.

I have provided *hand-mills* for each company, which are found to be exceedingly useful, as they are worked by the soldiers, who carry the meal to the depot, and receive bread in return. With this meal, you are enabled to husband your magazines, and have it in your power to remain much longer in camp than you could without such supply. Moreover, fewer escorts, and a smaller number of convoys will also be found sufficient.

On the subject of convoys, I must enlarge a little. The strength of escorts depends on the fear which you entertain of the enemy. Detachments of infantry are sent into the towns through which the convoys pass, to afford them a point of support. Large detachments to cover them are sometimes sent out, as was the case in Bohemia.

In all chequered countries, convoys should be escorted by the infantry, to which a few hussars may be added, in order to keep a lookout on the march, and inform themselves of all situations where the enemy may lie concealed.

My escorts have been formed of infantry in preference to cavalry even in a plain country, and in my own opinion, with very much advantage.

For what regards the minutiae of escorts, I refer you to my military regulation. The general of an army cannot be too anxious about the security of his convoys.

One good rule to attain this end is, to send troops forward for the purpose of occupying the defiles through which the convoy is to pass, and to push the escort a league in front towards the enemy. By this manoeuvre the convoys are masked, and arrive in security.

ARTICLE 3

Of Sutlers, Beer, and Brandy

When you have it in contemplation to make any enterprise on the enemy, the commissary must be ordered to get together all the beer and brandy that he can lay his hands on, that the army may not want these articles, at least for the first days. As soon as the army enters an enemy's country, all the brewers and distillers who are in the neighbourhood must immediately be put in requisition: the distillers, in particular, must be instantly set to work, that the soldier may not lose his dram, which he can very badly spare.

Protection must be afforded to the sutlers, especially in a country whose inhabitants are fled, and where provisions cannot be had for money. At such a time we are justified in not being over nice with respect to the peasantry.

The sutlers and women must be sent out in search of vegetables and cattle. The price of provisions is, however, a matter that requires much attention, as the soldier ought to be allowed to purchase at a reasonable price, and at the same time the sutler should derive an honest profit.

It may here be added, that the soldier receives *gratis* during a campaign two pounds of bread per day, and two pounds of flesh per week. It is an indulgence which the poor fellows richly deserve, especially in Bohemia, where the country is but little better than a desert.

Convoys for the army should ever be followed by herds of cattle, for the support and nourishment of the soldier.

ARTICLE 4

Of Dry and Green Forage.

Oats, barley, hay, chopped straw, &c. compose what is called *dry* forage, and are carried to the magazine. If the oats be either fusty or mouldy, the horses will contract the *mange* and *farcy*, and be so weakened as to be unserviceable even at the opening of a campaign. Chopped straw is given because it is the custom, though it serves but barely to fill the belly.

The first object in collecting forage and carrying it to the magazine is, either to get the start of the enemy at the opening of a campaign, or to be prepared for some distant enterprise. But an army can seldom venture to move far from its magazines, as long as the horses are obliged to live on dry forage, on account of the inconvenience of moving it, as a whole province is sometimes unable to furnish a sufficient number of carriages. And in general, these are not the methods that we employ in an offensive war, unless there are no rivers, by means of which the forage can be transported.

During the campaign in Silesia, all my cavalry lived on dry forage, but we only marched from Strehla to Schwiednitz, (where there was a magazine), and from thence to Cracau, where we were in the neighbourhood of the Brieg and the Oder.

When any enterprise is about to take place in the winter, the cavalry should carry with them forage for five days, well bound together on their horses. If Bohemia or Moravia are to be the scene of action, you must wait the arrival of spring, unless you mean to destroy all your cavalry. We forage in the fields for corn and vegetables as long as any remain there, and after harvest in the villages.

When we encamp on a spot where we mean to make some stay, an account should be taken of the forage; and when its quantity be ascertained, a regular distribution of it should be made according to the number of days which we intend to remain.

All large foraging parties are escorted by a body of cavalry, the strength of which is proportioned to the vicinity of the enemy, and the fear which you entertain of him. Foraging is sometimes earned on by the wings, or even the whole of an army.

The foragers always assemble on the road which they intend takings either on the wings, in front, or in the rear of the army.

The advanced guard is composed of hussars, who are followed by the cavalry in a plain country, but in irregular situations, the infantry go before them. The advanced guard is to precede the march of about a fourth part of the foragers, who are to be followed by a detachment of the escort, partly horse and partly foot; then another party of foragers, followed by a detachment of troops, and after them, the remainder in the same order. The march of the rear guard is to be closed by a troop of hussars, who will form the rear of the whole column.

It is to be remembered, that in all escorts the infantry take their cannon with them, and the foragers their swords and carbines.

When arrived at the spot where they intend foraging, a chain is to be formed, and the infantry posted near the villages, behind the hedges, and in the hollow ways. Troops of cavalry joined with infantry should be formed into a reserve, and placed in the centre to be ready to support any point where the enemy may endeavour to make an impression. The hussars are to skirmish with the enemy, in order to amuse them and draw them off from the forage. As soon as the enclosure is complete, the foragers divide the ground by regiments. Great care must be taken by the officers commanding, that the trusses be made very large, and bound well together.

When the horses are laden, the foragers are to return to camp by troops, protected by small escorts, and as soon as they have all left the ground, the troops of the chain are to assemble and form the rear guard, followed by the hussars.

The method of foraging in villages differs from the foregoing only in this instance, *viz.* the infantry are posted round the village, and the cavalry behind them in a situation where they may be able to act. Villages are to be foraged one by one, to prevent the troops of the chain from being too much dispersed.

In mountainous countries, foraging becomes an arduous business, and on such occasions the greatest part of the escorts must be composed of infantry and hussars.

When we are encamped near the enemy, and intend remaining there some time, we must endeavour to secure the forage which is between the two camps. After that, we are to forage for two leagues round, beginning with the most distant fields, and preserving those that are near home till the last. If no stay be intended, we forage in the camp and in the neighbourhood,

When it becomes an object to secure a large quantity of green forage, I would rather send the parties out *twice*, than occupy too great an extent of country at once. By this means you will preserve your chain more snug and compact, and the foragers will be in much greater security: whereas if too great a space be occupied, the chain must consequently be weakened and rendered liable to be forced.

ARTICLE 5

Of the Knowledge of a Country

The knowledge of a country is to be attained in two ways; the first (and that with which we ought to begin) is, by a careful and studious examination of a map of the country which is intended to be the scene of war, and by marking on it very distinctly the names of all the rivers, towns, and mountains that are of any consequence.

Having by this means gained a general idea of the country, we must proceed to a more particular and minute examination of it, to inform ourselves of the directions of the high roads, the situation of the towns, whether by a little trouble they can be made tenable, on what side to attack them if they are possessed by the enemy, and what number of troops are necessary for their defence.

We should also be provided with plans of the fortified towns, that we may be acquainted with their strength, and what are their most assailable parts. The course and depth of the large rivers should also be ascertained, how far they are navigable, and if shallow enough at any points to allow of being forded. It should also be known, what rivers are impassable in spring and dry in summer. This sort of enquiry must extend likewise to the marshes of any consequence that may be in the country.

In a flat, smooth country, the fertile parts should be distinguished from those that are not so, and we must be well acquainted with all the marches that either the enemy or ourselves can undertake, to pass from one great city or river to another. It will be necessary also to break up those camps, which are liable to be taken on that route.

A flat, open country can be reconnoitred presently, but the view is so confined in that which is woody and mountainous, that it becomes a business of much difficulty.

In order, therefore, to procure intelligence so highly important, we must ascend the heights, taking the map with us, and also some of the elders of the neighbouring villages, such as huntsmen and shepherds. If there be one mountain higher than another, *that* must be ascended, to gain an idea of a country which we wish to discover.

We must gain a knowledge of the roads, pot only to be satisfied in how many columns we may march, but also that we may be enabled to plan a variety of projects, and be informed how we may reach the enemy's camp and force it, should any be established in the neighbourhood, or how place ourselves on his flank, should he alter his position.

One of the most material objects is, to reconnoitre situations that, in case of necessity, may serve as camps of defence, as well as a field of battle, and the posts that may be occupied by the enemy.

A just idea must be formed of all these matters of intelligence, as well as of the most considerable posts, the valleys, chief defiles, and all the advantageous situations which the country affords: and we must seriously reflect on every operation that may take place, so that by being prepared beforehand with a plan of arrangements, we may not be embarrassed when called into action.

These reflections should be well connected, and maturely digested, with all the care and patience that an object of so much consequence requires; and unless we can arrange the matter to our satisfaction the first time, we must try it over again and again till we have got it perfect.

It is a general rule in the choice of all camps, whether for offence or defence, that both wood and water be near at hand, that the front be close and well covered, and the rear perfectly open.

If circumstances forbid the examination of a country in the manner laid down, clever, intelligent officers should be sent thither under any kind of excuse, or even in disguise if necessary. They are to be. well informed of the nature of the observations which they are to make, and at their return, the remarks which they have made on the camps and different situations are to be noted on a map; but when we can make use of our own eyes, we ought never to trust to those of other people.

ARTICLE 6

Of the *Coup D'Œil*

The *coup d'œil* may be reduced, properly speaking, to two points; the first of which is the hating abilities to judge how many troops at certain extent of country can contain. This talent can only be acquired by practice, for after having laid out several camps, the eye will gain so exact an idea of space, that you win seldom make any material mistake in your calculations.

The other, and by far the most material point, is to be able to distinguish at first sight all the advantages of which any given space of ground is capable. This art is to be acquired and even brought to perfection, though a man be not absolutely born with a military genius.

Fortification, as it possesses rules that are applicable to all situations of an army, is undoubtedly the basis and foundation of this *coup d'œil*. Every defile, marsh, hollow way, and even the smallest eminence, win be converted by a skilful general, to some advantage.

Two hundred different positions may sometimes be taken up in the space of two square leagues, of which an intelligent general knows how to select that which is the most advantageous. In the first place, he will ascend even the smallest eminences to discover and reconnoitre the ground; and assisted by the same rules of fortification, he will be enabled to find out the weak part of the enemy's order of battle. If time permit, the general would do well to *pace* over the ground, when he has determined on his general position.

Many other advantages may also be derived from the same roles of fortification, such as, the manner of occupying heights, and how to choose them, that they may not be commanded by others; in what manner the wings are to be supported, that the flanks may be well covered; how to take up positions that may be defended, and avoid those which a man of reputation cannot, without great risk, maintain. These rules will also enable him to discover where the enemy is weakest, either by having taken an unfavourable position, distributed his force without judgment, or from the slender means of defence which he derives from his situation. I am led by these reflections to explain in what manner troops ought to be distributed so as to make the most of their ground.

Article 7

Of the Distribution of Troops

Though the knowledge and choice of ground are very essential points, it is of no less importance that we know bow to profit by such advantages, so that the troops may be placed in situations that are proper and convenient for them.

Our cavalry, being designed to act with velocity, can only be made use of on a plain, whereas the infantry may be employed in every possible variety of ground. Their fire is for defence, and their bayonet for attack.

We always begin by the defensive, as much caution is necessary for the security of a camp, where the vicinity of the enemy may at any moment bring on an engagement.

The greater part of the orders of battle now existing are of ancient date: we tread in the steps of our ancestors without regulating matters according to the nature of the ground, and hence it is that a false and erroneous application so often takes place.

The whole of an army should be placed in order of battle agreeably to the nature of ground which every particular part of it requires. The plain is chosen for the cavalry, but this is not all which regards them; for if the plain be only a thousand yards in fronts and bounded by a wood in which we suppose the enemy to have thrown some infantry, under whose fire their cavalry can rally, it will then become necessary to change the disposition, and place them at the extremities of the wings of the infantry, that they may receive the benefit of their support.

The whole of the cavalry is sometimes placed on one of the wings, or in the second line: at other times, their wings are closed by one or two brigades of infantry.

Eminences, churchyards, hollow ways, and wide ditches are the most advantageous situations for an army. If, in the disposition of our troops, we know how to take advantage of these circumstances, we never need to fear being attacked.

If your cavalry be posted with a morass in its front, it is impossible that it can render you any service: and if it be placed too near a wood, the enemy may have troops there, who may throw them into disorder and pick them off with their muskets, whilst they are deprived of every possible means of defence. Your infantry will be exposed to the same inconveniences if they are advanced too far on a plain with their flanks not secured, for the enemy will certainly take advantage of such error, and make their attack on that side where they are unprotected.

The nature of the ground must invariably be our rule of direction. In a mountainous country I should place my cavalry in the second line, and never use them in the first line except they could act to advantage, unless it be a few squadrons to fall on the flank of the enemy's infantry who may be advancing to attack me.

It is a general rule in all well-disciplined armies, that a reserve of cavalry be formed if we are on a plain; but where the country is chequered and intersected, this reserve is formed of infantry, with the addition of some hussars and dragoons.

The great art of distributing troops on the field is, so to place them, that all have room to act and be uniformly useful. Villeroi, who perhaps was not well acquainted with this rule, deprived himself of the assistance of the whole of his left wing on the plain of Ramillies, by having posted them behind a morass, where it was morally impossible that they could manoeuvre, or render any sort of support to his right wing.

ARTICLE 8

Of Camp

To be convinced that your camp be well chosen, you must discover, whether a trifling movement of yours will oblige the enemy to make one of greater consequence, or if after one march, he be under the necessity of making others. They who have the least occasion to more, are certainly the best situated.

The choice of situation for a camp should rest entirely with the general of an army, as it often becomes the field of battle, and the success of his enterprises so materially depends upon it.

As there are many observations to be made on this subject, I shall enter into it very particularly, saying nothing with respect to the method of placing troops in camp, but referring you on that head to my *military regulation*.

I now proceed to speak only of affairs of consequence, and of matters that more immediately concern the general himself.

All camps are designed to answer two purposes, defence and attack. The first class consists of those camps in which an army assembles where the sole object is the convenience and accommodation of the

Auf der Zeichnung in dem Buche Kön:
Preuss. General-Stab, welche gegenw:
Fig. als Hauptquelle hat dienen müssen
findet sich kein Fahnenschuh dargestellt.

troops. They ought to be encamped in small bodies near the magazine, but so situate that they may readily be assembled in order of battle.

Camps of this kind are generally formed at such a distance from the enemy as to be free from all alarm. The King of England, who neglected this caution, and imprudently encamped himself on the bank of the Mein opposite the French Army, ran a very great risk of being defeated at Dettinghen.

The first rule to be observed in the marking out a camp is, that both wood and water be at no great distance.

It is our custom to entrench camps, in the manner of the Romans, not only to secure ourselves against any enterprise which the numerous light troops of the enemy may attempt against us, but also to prevent desertion.

I have constantly observed, that fewer men have left us when the *redans*, (fleche, or angular entrenchment, like an arrow), were joined by two lines that extended all round the camp, than when this caution has been neglected. This is a serious fact, however ridiculous or trifling it may appear.

Camps of repose are those, where we expect forage; on some occasions they are designed to watch the enemy, who have as yet made no movements, that we may be regulated by their manoeuvre. As relaxation is the only object in camps of this nature, they should be rendered secure by being in the rear of a large river or morass, or in short by any means that will render their front inaccessible. Of this description was our camp at Strehla.

If the brooks and rivers in front of the camp are too shallow, dams must be employed in order to deepen them.

Though there be no dread of the enemy to annoy us in camps of this kind, the general of an army must nevertheless on no account be idle. The leisure which he now has must be employed in paying attention to the troops, and re-establishing the usual discipline. He must examine if the service be carried on in strict conformity to order, if the officers on guard are attentive and well informed of the duties of their situation, and if the rules which I have laid down for the posting of cavalry and infantry guards be properly; and strictly observed.

The infantry should go through their exercise three times a week, and the recruits once every day: on some occasions also entire corps may perform their manoeuvres together.

The cavalry must likewise go through their evolutions, unless they are employed in foraging; and the general, knowing the exact strength of each corps, should take particular care that the recruits and young horses be well drilled. He must also frequently visit the lines, commending those officers who pay attention to their troops, and severely rebuking those who appear to have neglected them, for it is not to be supposed that a large army can be *self*-animated. It will ever abound with idlers and malingers, who require the general's attention to be put in motion and be obliged to do their duty.

Very great utility will be derived from camps of this sort, if they be employed in the manner which I have recommended, and the succeeding campaign will prove the good effects of their discipline and order.

We form our encampment, or we forage, near to the enemy, or at a considerable distance from him—I shall only speak of the former, where it is necessary that we make choice of the most fertile spots, and encamp in a situation which art or nature has rendered formidable.

When foraging camps are situate near the enemy, they should be very difficult of access, as foraging parties are regarded as detachments sent out against the enemy.

These parties may consist of a sixth part, or even the half of an army. It would afford fine amusement to the enemy, if they were able on these occasions to attack us to our disadvantage, and it would certainly happen, but for the well-chosen situation of our camp. But though the position be very good, and apparently there be nothing to fear from the enemy, there are, notwithstanding, other cautions which are by no means to be neglected. The most rigid secrecy must be observed both in regard to the time and place of foraging, nor should even the general who is to command on the occasion be acquainted with these circumstances till a late hour in the preceding evening.

We should send out as many detached parties as possible, to be more certainly informed of any movements which the enemy may make: and unless prevented by reasons that are very material, we may, to save trouble, forage on the same day that they do. We are not, however, to place too much confidence in this circumstance, as the enemy, by being apprised of our design, may countermand the order for foraging, and attack the main body.

The camp of Prince Charles of Lorraine under Kônigingraetz was inaccessible by nature, and extremely convenient for the purposes of foraging. That which we occupied at Cholm was made strong by art, *viz.* by the abbatis which I ordered to be thrown up on our right wing and the redoubts which were in front of the infantry camp.

We entrench a camp, when it is our intention to lay siege to a place, to defend a difficult pass, and supply the defects of situation by throwing up works so as to be secure from every insult on the part of the enemy.

The rules which a general had to observe in the formation of all entrenchments are, to make a good choice of situation, and to take advantage of every marsh, river, inundation, and abbatis which may serve to render the extent of his entrenchments more difficult. They had better be too small than too large, for the progress of the enemy is not checked by the entrenchments themselves, but by the troops who defend them.

I would not wish to make entrenchments, unless I could line them with a chain, of battalions, and had also at my disposal a reserve of infantry that could be moved to any point as occasion might require. Abbatis are no longer of service than whilst they are defended by infantry.

The chief attention should be paid to the proper support of the lines of contravallation, which generally end in a river; and in such case the *fossè* should be carried some length into the river, and be so deepened as not to allow of being forded. If this precaution be neglected, you run the hazard of having your flank turned. It is necessary that you be abundantly supplied with provisions before you sit down behind the lines to besiege any place.

The flanks of entrenchments should be particularly strong, nor should there be a single point which the enemy might attack without being exposed to four or five cross fires. Infinite care and caution are required in the formation of entrenchments which are designed to defend the passes and defiles of mountains. The support of the flanks is here most essentially necessary, to accomplish which, redoubts are formed on the two wings: sometimes the whole entrenchment itself is made up of redoubts, so that the troops who defend it are in no danger of being turned.

Intelligent generals are well informed how to oblige the enemy to attack those points where the work is made strongest by the ditch being widened, deepened, and lined with *pallisadoes, chevaux de frize* placed at the entrances, the parapet made *cannon-proof,* and pits dug in the places that are most exposed.

But for the covering of a siege, I would always prefer an army of observation to an entrenched camp, and for this plain reason, because we are taught by experience that the old method is not to be depended on.

The Prince of Condé saw his entrenchment which was before Arras forced by Turenne, and Condé (if I am not mistaken) forced that which Turenne had formed before Valenciennes—since that period, neither of these great masters in the military art have made any use of them, but, to cover a siege, have always employed armies of observation.

I shall now treat of defensive camps, which are only strong by situation, and intended solely to be secure from the attacks of the enemy.

To render these situations equal to the purposes for which they are designed, it is necessary, that the front and both flanks be of equal strength, and the rear perfectly free and open. Of such nature are those heights, whose front is very extensive, and whose flanks are covered by marshes, as was the camp of Prince Charles of Lorraine at Marschwitz, where the front was covered by a marshy river, and the flanks by lakes; or like that which we occupied at Konopist in the year 1744.

We may also shelter ourselves under the protection of some fortified place, as was done by the Marshal de Neipperg, who, after being defeated at Mollwitz, took up an excellent position under the walls of Neiss. As long as a general can maintain his post in camps of this kind, he will be secure from attack; but as soon as the enemy is in motion with a view of turning him, he will no longer be able to remain. His arrangements should therefore be so settled before-hand, that if the enemy succeed in their attempt to turn him, he may have nothing to do but fall back, and take up another strong position in the rear.

Bohemia abounds in camps of this description, and as the country is so chequered by nature, we are often obliged to occupy some of them against our inclination.

I must again repeat how necessary it is for a general to be on his guard, lest he be led, by a bad choice of posts, into errors that cannot be remedied, or gets himself shut up in a *cul de sac*, or in a situation from which he has no means of escaping but by a narrow defile. For if he have a clever enemy to deal with, he will be so closely pent up, and so completely prevented from fighting by the nature of the ground, as to be obliged to submit to the greatest indignity which a soldier can suffer, that of laying down his arms without the power of defending himself.

In camps that are intended to cover a country, the strength of the place itself is not the object of attention, but those points which are liable to attack, and by means of which the enemy may penetrate.

These should all be surrounded by the camp. Not that it is necessary to occupy every opening by which the enemy may advance upon us, but *that one* only which would lead to his desired point, and that situation which affords as security, and from which we have it in our power to alarm him. In short, we should occupy that post, which will oblige the enemy to take circuitous routes, and enable us, by small movements, to disconcert all his projects.

The camp at Newstadt defends the whole of the Lower Silesia against the attacks of an army that may be in Moravia. The proper position to take up, is to have the city of Neustadt and the river in front, and if the enemy shew a design to pass between Ottmachau and Glatz, we have only to move between Neiss and Ziegenhals, and there take up an advantageous camp which will cut them off from Moravia.

For the same reason the enemy will not dare to stir on the side of Cosel, for by placing myself between Troppau and Jaegerndorff (where these are many very excellent positions), I cut him off from his convoys.

There is another camp of equal importance between Liebau and Schaemberg, which secures all Lower Silesia against Bohemia.

In all these positions, the rules which I have laid down ought to be observed, as far as circumstances will allow. I must yet add one more, which is, that when you have a river in front, you never allow tents to be pitched on the ground which you intend for the field of battle at a greater distance than half musket-shot from the front of the camp.

The frontier of the electorate of Brandenberg is a country which no camp can cover, as it has six leagues of plain ground which is open the whole way. To defend it against Saxony, it is necessary to be possessed of Wittenberg, and either encamp there or adopt the plan of the expedition which took place there in the winter of the year 1745. The camp at Werben covers and defends all that part which is on the side of the country of Hanover.

The front and flanks of a camp for offence must be always closed; for unless the flanks, which are the weakest part of an army, are well closed, you have nothing to expect from your troops. This was the fault of our camp at Czaslaw, before the battle, of the year 1742.

The village houses which are on the wings, or in the front of our camp, are always occupied by troops, except on fighting days, when they are called in, lest by the enemy's setting fire to such badly-constructed wooden buildings (as our own cottages and those of our neighbours generally are) the men may also be destroyed. There may, however, be an exception to this rule, when any *stone* houses are in the villages, or any churchyards which do not communicate with wooden buildings.

But as it is our constant principle to attack, and not act on the defensive, this kind of post should never be occupied except it be at the head of the army, or in front of its wings; in such situation it will afford much protection to our troops in the attack, and prove of great annoyance to the enemy during the action.

It is also a circumstance of material import, that the depth of the small rivers or marshes which are in front or on the flanks of our camp be well ascertained, lest by the rivers being fordable, or the marshes practicable, you discover too late that you hare trusted to a false point of defence.

Villars was beaten at Malplaquet by conceiving that the marsh on his right was impracticable, which proved to be only a dry meadow, which our troops passed to take him in flank. Everything should be examined by our own eyes, and no attentions of this nature treated on any account as matters of indifference.

ARTICLE 9

How to secure a Camp

The front of the first line must be defended by the regiments of infantry, and if a river be there, piquets must be posted on its banks. The rear of the camp is to be guarded by piquets from the second line. These piquets are to be covered by *redans*, joined by slight entrenchments, by means of which the camp will be entrenched after the manner of the Romans. We must occupy the villages which are on the wings, or even to the distance of half a league from thence, if they serve to defend any other passages.

The cavalry guards are to be posted agrees ably to the rules laid down in my military regulation. We seldom had more than 300 *maitres de garde*, (private dragoons on guard), amongst 80 squadrons, unless we were very near to the enemy, as when we marched to Schwiednitz between the Battle of Hohen-Friedberg, and again when we marched into Lusatia in order to go to Naumbourg. These advanced guards should be composed of all sorts of troops; for example, 2000 hussars, 1500 dragoons, and 2000 grenadiers. The general who has the command of bodies of men that are advanced, should be a man of sound understanding, and as it is his object to gain intelligence, not expose himself to action, his camps should be chosen with judgment, having in their front either woods or defiles with which he is well acquainted. He must also send out frequent patrols for the purpose of gaining information, that he may know at every instant what is going forward in the camp of the enemy.

If in the meantime you employ the hussars who remain with you to patrol in the rear and on the wings of the camp, you have taken all possible precautions to be guarded against any hostile enterprises.

Should a considerable body of troops endeavour to slide in between you and your rear guard, you may be assured that they have formed some design against it, and you are therefore to hasten to its support.

To conclude all that, I have to say on this subject, it must be added, that if those generals who canton their troops wish to be free from danger and alarm, they should only occupy those villages which are between the two lines.

ARTICLE 10

In what Manner and for what Reason
We are to send out Detachments.

It is only repeating an ancient maxim in war to say, "*that he who divides his force, will be beaten in detail.*" If you are about to give battle, strain every nerve to get together as many troops as you possibly can, for they never can be employed to better purpose. Almost every general who has neglected this rule, has found ample reason to repent of it.

Albemarle's detachment, which was beaten at Oudenarde, lost the great Eugene the whole campaign; and Gen. Stahremberg was beaten at the Battle of Villa Viciosa in Spain, by being separated from the English troops.

Detachments have also proved very fatal to the Austrians in the latter campaigns that they have made in Hungary. The Prince of Hildbourghausen was defeated at Banjaluka, and General Wallis suffered a check on the banks of the Timok. The Saxons also were beaten at Kesselsdorf, for want of having joined Prince Charles, as they could have done. *I* should have been defeated at Sohr, and deservedly too, if presence of mind in my generals, and valour in my troops, had not rescued me from such misfortune. It may be asked, are we then never to send, out detachments? My reply is, that it is a business of so delicate a nature, as never to be hazarded but on the most pressing necessity, and for reasons of the utmost importance.

When you are acting *offensively*, detachments ought never to be employed, and even though you are in an open country, and have some places in your possession, no more troops are to be spared than are barely sufficient to secure your convoys.

Whenever war is made in Bohemia or Moravia, necessity requires that troops be sent out to insure the arrival of provisions. Encampments must be formed on the chain of mountains which the convoys are obliged to pass, and remain there till you have collected provisions for some months, and are possessed of some strong place in the enemy's country that will serve as a depot.

Whilst these troops are absent on detachments, you are to occupy advantageous camps, and wait for their return.

The advanced guard is not reckoned as a detachment, because it should ever be near the army, and not ventured on any account too near the enemy.

It sometimes happens, that when we arc acting on the defensive, we are forced to make detachments. Those which I had in Upper Silesia were in perfect safety by confining themselves, as I have already observed, to the neighbourhood of fortified places.

Officers who have the command of detachments, should be men of prudence and resolution, for though they receive *general* instructions from their chief, it remains for *themselves* to consult on the propriety of advancing or retreating, as occasion may require.

When the force of the opponents is too strong, they should fall back, but on the other hand, they should well know how to take advantage, if the superiority happen to be on their own sides.

If the enemy approach by night, they will sometimes retire, and whilst they are supposed to be put to flight, return briskly to the charge and defeat them.

No regard whatever is to be paid to the light troops.

The first thing to be attended to by an officer who commands a detachment, is his own safety, and when that is secured, he is at liberty to form schemes against the enemy. To ensure rest to himself, he must keep his adversary constantly awake, by continually contriving plans against him, and if he succeed in two or three instances, the enemy will be obliged to keep on the defensive.

If these detachments be near the army, they will establish a communication with it by means of some town or neighbouring wood.

In a war of *defence*, we are naturally induced to make detachments. Generals of little experience are anxious to preserve everything, whilst the man of intelligence and enterprise regards only the grand point, in hopes of being able to strike some great stroke, and suffers patiently a small evil that may secure him against one of more material consequence.

The army of the enemy should be the chief object of our attention, it's designs must be discovered, and opposed as vigorously as possible. In the year 1745 we abandoned Upper Silesia to the ravages of the Hungarians, that we might be better enabled to thwart the intentions of Prince Charles of Lorraine, and we made no detachments until we had defeated his army. When that was done. General Nassau in fifteen days cleared the whole of Upper Silesia of the Hungarians.

It is a custom with some generals to detach troops when they are about to make an attack, to take the enemy in the rear during the action, but much danger attends a movement of this kind, as the detachments generally lose their road, and arrive either too early or too late. The detachment which Charles XII. sent out on the evening before the Battle of Pultawa lost its way, and was the cause of the army's being beaten. Prince Eugene's design, of surprising Cremona failed also from the too late arrival of the detachment of the Prince of Vaudemont, which was intended to attack the gate of Po.

Detachments should never take place on the day of battle, unless it be in the manner of Turenne near Colmar, where he presented his first line to the army of the Elector Frederick William, whilst the second line passing through defiles attacked him in flank and routed him. Or we may copy the example of the Marshal de Luxembourg at the Battle of Fleury, in the year 1690, who posted a body of infantry in some high corn on the Prince of Waldeck's flank, and by that manoeuvre gained the battle.

After a victory, but never till then, troops may be detached for the protection of convoys, but even in this case they should not proceed a greater length than half a league from the army.

I shall conclude this article by saying, that detachments which weaken the army one half, or even a third part, are excessively dangerous, and strongly to be disapproved.

ARTICLE 11

Of the Tricks and Stratagems of War

In war, the skin of a fox is at times as necessary as that of the lion, for cunning may succeed when force fails. Since, therefore, force may at one time be repelled by force, and at another be obliged to yield to

Frühere Uniform
bis 1775.

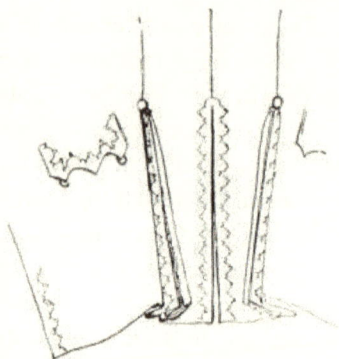

stratagem, we ought to be well acquainted with the use of both, that we may on occasion adopt either.

I have no wish to recite here the almost infinite list of stratagems, for they have all the same end in view, which is, to oblige the enemy to make unnecessary marches in favour of our own designs. Our real intentions are to be studiously concealed, and the enemy misled by our affecting plans which we have no wish to execute.

When our troops are on the point of assembling, we counter-march them in a variety of ways, to alarm the enemy, and conceal from him the spot where we *really* wish to assemble and force a passage.

If there be fortresses in the country, we chose to encamp in a situation that threatens three or four places at the same time. Should the enemy think proper to throw troops into *all* these places, the consequence will be, that his force will be so weakened, that we shall have a good opportunity of falling on him: but if *one* point only has been the object of his attention, we may lay siege to that which is the most defenceless.

If the object be to pass a river, or be possessed of some post of importance, you must withdraw to a great distance both from the post and from the spot where you mean to pass, in order to entice the enemy after you. And when everything is arranged and your march concealed, you are to betake yourself suddenly to the settled point and possess yourself of it.

If you wish to come to an action, md the enemy seems disposed to avoid it, you must appear to be in dread of the force which is opposed to you, or spread a report that your army is much weakened. We played this game before the Battle of Hohen-Friedberg. I caused all the roads to be repaired as if I meant, at the approach of Prince Charles, to march to Breslau in four columns: his self-confidence sec-onding my design, he followed me into the plain, and was defeated.

Sometimes we contract the dimensions of the camp, to give it the appearance of weakness, and send out small detachments, (that we affect to be of great consequence), in order that the enemy may hold us cheap, and neglect an opportunity which he might improve. In the campaign of 1745, if it had been my intention to take Kônigingraetz and Pardubitz, I had only to make two marches through the county of Glatz on the side of Moravia, as that would certainly have alarmed Prince Charles and brought him thither, to defend the place from which, after leaving Bohemia, he drew all his provisions. You will be sure of creating jealousy in the enemy, if you threaten places that either communicate with the capitol or serve as depots for his provisions.

If we have no inclination to fight, we put a bold face upon the business, and give out that we are much stronger than we really are. Austria is a famous school for this sort of manoeuvre, for with them the art is brought to its greatest perfection.

By keeping up a bold and determined appearance, you give the idea of wishing to engage, and occasion a report to be circulated that you are meditating some very bold and daring enterprise: by means of which the enemy, in dread of the consequences of an attack, will frequently remain on the defensive.

It is an essential object in a war of *defence*, to know how to make a good choice of posts, and to maintain them to the last extremity: when forced to retire, the second line begins to move, followed insensibly by the first, and as you have defiles in your front, the enemy will not be able to take advantage of you in the retreat.

Even during the retreat, the positions that are taken up should be so oblique as to keep the enemy as much as possible in the dark. The more he endeavours to discover your designs, the more he will be alarmed, whilst you indirectly obtain the object of your wishes.

Another stratagem of war is, to shew to the enemy a front of very great extent, and if he mistake a false attack for a real one, he will inevitably be defeated.

By means of tricks also, we oblige the enemy to send out detachments, and when they are marched, take the opportunity of falling on him.

The best stratagem is, to lull the enemy into security at the time when the troops are about to disperse and go into winter quarters, so that by retiring, you may be enabled to advance on them to some good purpose. With this view, the troops should be so distributed, as to assemble again very readily, in order to force the enemy's quarters. If this measure succeed, you may recover in a fortnight the misfortunes of a whole campaign.

Peruse with attention the two last campaigns of Turenne, for they are the *chefs d'œuvres* of the stratagems of this age.

The schemes which our ancestors employed in war are now only in use amongst the light troops, whose practice it is to form ambuscades, and endeavour by a pretended flight to draw the enemy into a defile, that they may cut them in pieces. The generals of the present day seldom manage their matters so badly as to be taken in by such contrivances. Nevertheless, Charles XIL was betrayed at Pultawa through the treachery of one of the Cossac chiefs. The same accident also befell Peter I. on the Pruth, owing to the misconduct of a prince of that country. Both these men had promised a supply of provisions which it was not in their power to furnish.

As the method of making war by parties and detachments is fully laid down in my *Military Regulation*, I refer to that work all those who wish to refresh their memories, as it is a subject on which I have nothing farther to advance.

To be informed of the method to oblige the enemy to make detachments, we have only to read over the glorious campaign of 1690, made by the Marshal de Luxembourg against the King of England, which concluded with the Battle of *Neerwinde*.

ARTICLE 12

Of Spies, how they are to be employed on every Occasion, and
in what Manner we are to learn Intelligence of the Enemy.

If we were acquainted beforehand with the intentions of the enemy, we should always be more than a match for him even with an inferior force. It is an advantage which all generals are anxious to procure, but very few obtain.

Spies may be divided into several classes: 1st, common people who choose to be employed in such concern; 2ndly, double spies; 3rdly, spies of consequence; 4thly, those who are *compelled* to take up the unpleasant business.

The common gentry, *viz.* peasants, mechanics, priests, &c. which are sent into the camp, can only be employed to discover *where* the enemy is: and their reports are generally so incongruous and obscure, as rather to increase our uncertainties than lessen them.

The intelligence of deserters is, for the most part, not much more to be depended on. A soldier knows very well what is going forward in his own regiment, but nothing farther. The hussars being detached in front, and absent the greatest part of their time from the army, are often ignorant on which side it is encamped. Nevertheless, their reports must be committed to paper, as the only means of turning them to any advantage.

Double spies are used to convey false intelligence to the enemy. There was an Italian at Schmiedeberg, who acted as a spy to the Austrians, and being told by us, that when the enemy approached we should retire to Breslau, he posted with the intelligence to Prince

Charles of Lorraine, who narrowly escaped being taken in by it.

The post-master at Versailles was a long time in the pay of Prince Eugene. This unfortunate fellow opened the letters and orders which were sent from court to the generals, and transmitted a copy of them to Prince Eugene, who generally received them much earlier than the commanders of the French Army.

Luxembourg had gained over to his interest a secretary of the King of England, who informed him of all that passed. The king discovered it, and derived every advantage from it that could be expected in an affair of such delicacy: he obliged the traitor to write to Luxembourg, informing him that the allied army would be out the day following on a large foraging party. The consequence was that the French very narrowly escaped being surprised at Steinquerque, and would have been cut to pieces if they had not defended themselves with extraordinary valour.

It would be very difficult to obtain such spies in a war against Austria: not that the Austrians are less alive to bribery than other people, but because their army is surrounded by such a cloud of light troops, who suffer no creature to pass without being well searched. This circumstance suggested to me the idea of bringing over some of their hussar officers, by means of whom a correspondence might be carried on in the following manner. It is a custom with hussars, when opposed to each other as skirmishing parties, to agree every now and then to a suspension of arms, which opportunity might be employed in conveying letters.

When we wish to gain intelligence of the enemy, or give him a false impression of our situation and circumstances, we employ a trusty soldier to go from our camp to that of the enemy, and report what we wish to have believed. He may also be made the bearer of hand-bills calculated to encourage desertion. Having completed his business, he may take a circuitous march and return to camp.

There is yet another way to gain intelligence of the enemy when milder methods fail, though I confess it to be a harsh and cruel practice. We find out a rich citizen who has a large family and good estate, and allow him a man who understands the language of the country dressed as a servant, whom we force him to take along with him into the enemy's camp, as his valet or coachman, under pretence of complaining of some injuries which he has received; he is to be threatened also at the same time, that if he does not return after a certain period, and bring the man with him, that his houses shall be burned, and his wife and children hacked in pieces. I was obliged to have recourse to this scheme at —— and it succeeded to my wish.

I must farther add, that in the payment of spies, we ought to be generous, even to a degree of extravagance. That man certainly deserves to be well rewarded, who risks his neck to do you service.

ARTICLE 13

Of certain Marks, by which the Intentions of the Enemy are to be discovered

The knowledge of the spot which the enemy has chosen as a depot for his provisions is the surest means of discovering his intentions before the campaign opens. For example, if the Austrians establish their magazines at Olmutz, we may be assured that they mean to attack Upper Silesia: if at Kônigingraetz, we may be convinced that part of Schweidnitz is threatened. When it was the wish of the Saxons to invade the frontier of the Electorate, their magazines marked their intended route, for they were established at Zittau, Görlitz, and at Guben, which are on the road leading to Crossen.

The first object of intelligence should be, on what side and in what situations the enemy means to fix his magazines.

The French played a double game, by forming depots on the Meuse and on the Scheld, in order to conceal their intentions.

When the Austrians are encamped, it is easy to discover when they intend moving, by their custom of cooking on the days of march. If, therefore, much smoke be perceived in their camp at five or six o'clock in the morning, you may take it for granted on that day they mean to move.

Whenever the Austrians intend fighting, all their strong detachments of light troops are called in; and when you have observed this, it behoves you to be very well upon your guard.

If you attack a post which is defended by their Hungarian troops, without being able to make any impression on it, you may be satisfied that the army is near at hand to support them.

If their light troops endeavour to post themselves between your army and the body of men which you have detached, you may be assured that the enemy has a design on that detachment, and your measures must be taken accordingly.—It must be added, that if the same general be always opposed to you, his designs will be readily discovered, and his plan of conduct very soon become familiar.

After mature reflection on the nature of the country which is the

Preussen.

Offizier.   Musketier.

Infanterie-Regiment Herzog Ferdinand von Braunschweig
(1806: No. 5).

1757.

scene of war, the state of the army which you command, the safety of the magazines, the strength of the fortified places, the means which the enemy may be able to employ in order to gain possession of them, the mischief which the light troops may do by posting themselves on your flanks, rear, and other parts, or if the enemy should employ them to make a diversion; I say, after having well deliberated on all these points, you may conclude that an intelligent enemy will attempt that enterprise which is likely to give you the greatest annoyance, at least that such will be his intention, to frustrate which your every effort must be exerted.

ARTICLE 14

Of our own Country, and that which is either Neutral or Hostile; of the Variety of Religions, and of the different Conduct which such Circumstances require

War may be carried on in three different kinds of country; either in our own territories, those belonging to neutral powers, or in the country of an enemy.

If glory were my only object, I would never make war but in my own country, by reason of its manifold advantage, as every man *there* acts as a spy, nor can the enemy stir a foot without being betrayed.

Detachments of any strength may boldly be sent out, and may practise in safety all the manoeuvres of which war is capable.

If the enemy have the advantage, every peasant turns soldier and lends a hand to annoy him, as was experienced by the Elector Frederick William after the Battle of Fehrbelin, where a greater number of Swedes was destroyed by the peasants than fell in the engagement. After the battle of Hohen-Friedberg, also, I observed that the *mountaineers* in Silesia brought into us the runaway Austrians in great abundance.

When war is carried on in a neutral country, the advantage seems to be equal, and the object of attention then is, to rival the enemy in the confidence and friendship of the inhabitants. To attain this end, the most exact discipline must be observed, marauding and every kind of plunder strictly forbidden, and its commission punished with exemplary severity. It may not be amiss also, to accuse the enemy of harbouring some pernicious designs against the country.

If we are in a protestant country, we wear the mask of protector of the *Lutheran* religion, and endeavour to make *fanatics* of the lower order of people, whose simplicity is not proof against our artifice.

43

In a Catholic country, we preach up toleration and moderation, constantly abusing the priests as the cause of all the animosity that exists between the different sectaries, although, in spite of their disputes, they all agree upon material points of faith.

The strength of the parties you may be required to send out, must depend on the confidence that, can be placed in the inhabitants of the country. In our country you may run every risk, but more caution, and circumspection are necessary in a neutral country, at least, till you are convinced of the friendly disposition of the whole, or the greatest part of the peasantry.

In a country that is entirely hostile, as Bohemia and Moravia, you are to hazard nothing, and never send out parties, for the reasons already mentioned, as the people there are not to be trusted any farther than you can see them. The greater part of the light troops are to be employed in guarding the convoys, for you are never to expect to gain the affection of the inhabitants of this country. The Hussites in the circle of Kônigingraetz are the only people that can be induced to render us any sort of service. The men of consequence there, though seemingly well-disposed towards us, are arrant traitors, nor are the priests or magistrates at all better. As their interest is attached to that of the house of Austria, whose views do not altogether clash with ours, we neither can nor ought repose any sort of confidence in them.

All that now remains for our management is *fanaticism*, to know how to inspire a nation with zeal for the liberty of religion, and hint to them in a guarded' manner, how much they are oppressed by their great men and priests. This may be said *to be moving heaven and hell for one's interest.*

Since these notes have been put together, the empress queen has materially increased the taxes in Bohemia and Moravia: advantage may be taken of this circumstance to gain the good-will of the people, especially if we flatter them that they shall be better treated if we become masters of the country.

ARTICLE 15
Of every Kind of March, which it can be necessary for an Army to make

An army moves for the purposes of advancing in an enemy's country, to take possession of an advantageous camp, join a reinforcement, give battle, or retire before the enemy.

When the camp is properly secured, the next object is, to reconnoitre the whole neighbourhood and every road that leads from it to camp, that we may be enabled to make the necessary arrangements, as a variety of circumstances may require.

With this view, and under various pretences we send out large detachments, accompanied by some engineers and quartermasters, who are to pry into every place that is capable of being occupied by troops. They are also to take up the situation of the country, and reconnoitre the roads by which the troops can march. A certain number of *chasseurs* should follow them, who are to observe the roads very attentively, that they may be able to lead the columns, provided that the general marches thither.

On their return, the aforesaid officers are to make their report concerning the situation of the camp, the roads that lead to it, the nature of the soil, the woods, mountains, and rivers that are situate thereabouts; and the general, being well informed of all these particulars, will make his dispositions accordingly. When the camp is not too near the enemy, the following arrangement may take place:—

I suppose that the camp may be approached in four different ways. The advanced guard, composed of six battalions of grenadiers, one regiment of infantry, two of dragoons, (consisting of five squadrons each), and two regiments of hussars, under the command of Mr. N. N. will depart at eight o'clock this evening. All the encampments of the army are to follow this advanced guard, which is to take their tents only with them, leaving their heavy baggage with the army.

These troops are to march four leagues in front, and occupy the defile, river, height, town, village, &c. which may be objects of attentioii, and wait there the arrival of the army, after which they are to enter into the camp which has been already marked out.

On the following morning the army, marching in four columns, is to move forward after the advanced guard: those men who have been posted as guards in the villages, filling in with their respective regiments. The cavalry of the two lines of the right wing, marching by its right, will form the first column: the infantry of the two lines of the right wing, marching by its right, will form the second: the infantry of the two lines of the left wing, filing by its right, will form the third; and the cavalry of the left wing, filing by its right, will form the fourth column.

The infantry regiments N. N. of the second line, and the three regiments of hussars under the command of Gen. N. N. will escort the baggage, which is to march in the rear of the two columns of infantry.

Van Guard.

Detach.t of Dragoons

1. Bat.n of Grenad.rs

5. Squad.n of Drag.

3.Bat.ns of Grenad.rs

5.Squad.ns of Drag.ns

2.Bat.ns of Grenad.rs

1 Reg.t of Infant.y

Grand Guard of Caval.y

Small Encamp.t

Grand Guard of Infant.y

Encampment

Pl.t

Four *aides-de-camp* are to command this party, who are to take particular care that the carriages follow each other in order, allowing as little interval as possible. If the general commanding the rear guard should be in want of support, he is immediately to apply to the commander in chief.

The *chasseurs* who have reconnoitred the roads, are to conduct the four columns.

A detachment of carpenters, with waggons laden with beams, joists, and planks, should precede each column, to throw bridges over the small rivers.

The heads of columns must be careful not to go before each other on the march.

The generals are to take care that the battalions march close to each other without allowing any intervals. Officers commanding divisions must be attentive in observing their distances.

When you have to pass a defile, the heads of columns must march very slowly, or halt now and then to allow the rear to recover its situation.

It is thus that the order of march is to be conducted.

When mountains, woods, or defiles are met with on the march, the columns are to be divided, and the head, which consists of the infantry, is to be followed by the cavalry, who will close the march.

If there be a plain in the centre, it is to be assigned to the cavalry, and the infantry, formed into columns on the two extremities, fire to traverse the wood; but this is only to be understood of a march which is made not too near the enemy. In *that* situation, we are content to place some battalions of grenadiers at the head of each column of cavalry, that they may preserve the order of battle.

The most certain way to insure the safe arrival of a reinforcement is, to march through a difficult road to meet it, and to retire from the enemy to avoid an engagement. By means of the superiority which you gain by the arrival of this succour, you will soon recover that ground) which you have, as it were, only *lent* to the enemy.

When we are obliged to march parallel to the enemy, it must be done in two lines, either by the right or by the left, and each line must form a column, with an advanced guard in front. In other respects, those rules which I have just laid down, may also here be employed.

All the marches which we made from Frankenberg to Hohen-Friedberg were directed in this manner, marching to the tight.

I prefer these dispositions to any others, because the army can

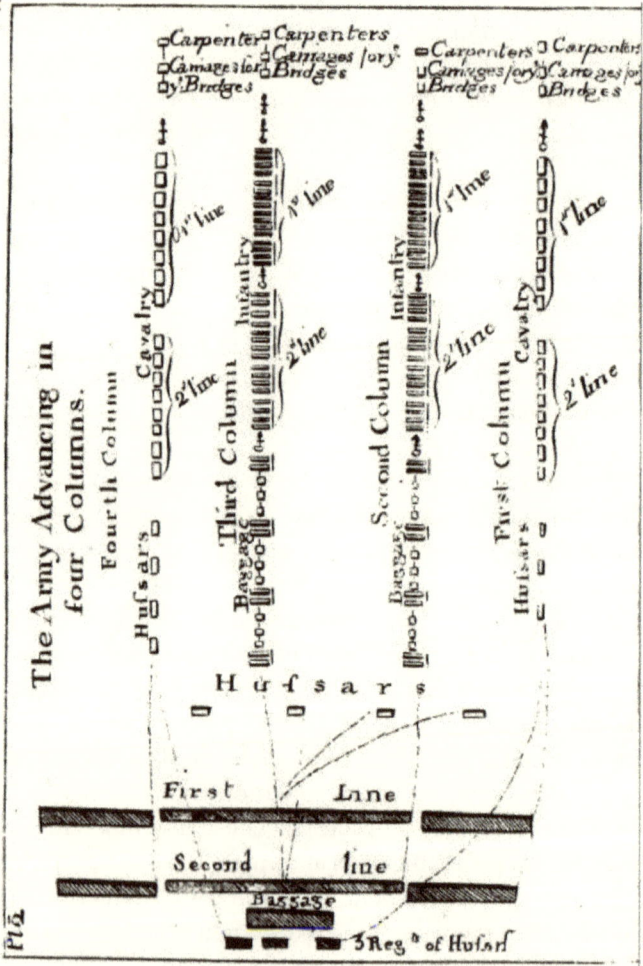

The Army Advancing in four Columns.

Carpenter Carpenters Carpenters Carpenters
Carriages for ye Carriages for ye Carriages for ye Carriages for
ye Bridges Bridges Bridges Bridges

Fourth Column

Cavalry
1st line
2d line

Third Column

Infantry
1st line
2d line

Baggage

Second Column

Infantry
1st line
2d line

Baggage

First Column

Cavalry
1st line
2d line

Hussars

Hussars

H u s s a r s

First   Line

Second   line

Baggage

3 Regd of Hussars

Pl 2.

be formed in order of battle by one to the right or one to the left, which is by much the readiest way of collecting them, and I would ever practise this method, if I had my choice in attacking the enemy, though I lost the advantage of it at Shorn and at Hohen-Friedberg. In this sort of march, care is to be taken that the flank be never shewn to the enemy.

When the enemy begins a march in preparation for an action, you are to disencumber yourself of all your heavy baggage, and send it under an escort to the nearest town. The advanced guard is then to be formed, and pushed forward to the distance of a short half league.

When the army marches in front against the enemy, care must be taken not only that the columns do not go before each other, but also that when they draw near to the field of battle, they extend themselves in such a manner, that the troops do not take up more or less ground than they will occupy when they are formed. This is a business of much difficulty, as some battalions are generally too much crowded, and others have too much ground allotted them.

Marching by lines is attended with no sort of inconvenience, and on that account has by me ever been preferred.

When we expect to be engaged upon a march, great precaution is required, and it is necessary that the general be very much upon his guard. He should reconnoitre the ground, without exposing himself, from point to point, so as to have an idea of different positions, if the enemy should come to attack him.

Steeples and heights are to be made use of in order to reconnoitre the ground, and the road which leads to them is to be cleared by light troops, detached from the advanced guard.

Retreats are generally conducted in the following manner: A day or two before we depart, the heavy baggage is got together, and sent away under a strong escort.

The number of columns is then to be determined by the number of roads that can be made use of, and the march of the troops regulated by the nature of the ground. In a plain, the advanced guard is formed by the cavalry; if it be a chequered country, that post belongs to the infantry. In a plain country, the army will march in four columns.

The infantry of the second line of the right wing, filing by its right, and followed by the second line of the cavalry of the same wing, will form the fourth column. The infantry of the first line of the right wing, filing by its right, will be followed by the first line cavalry of that wing, and form the third column.

Army Retreating in Four Columns

Right Wing
2ª Line of Infan.
2ª Line of Cav.ª
Hussars

Right Wing
1ª Line of Infan.
1ª Line of Cav.ª
Hussars

Left Wing
2ª Line of Infan.
2ª Line of Cav.ª
Hussars

Left Wing
1ª Line of Infan.
1ª Line of Cav.ª
Hussars

P.3

The infantry of the second line of the left wing, followed by the cavalry of the same line, will form the second column. The infantry of the first line of the left wing will be followed by the cavalry of the same line, forming together the first column.

In this manner the rear guard will be formed by the whole of the cavalry, which may be supported, for security sake, by the hussars of the army.

If, during the retreat, it be necessary to pass any defiles, the infantry must occupy them the evening before we depart, and be so posted as to cover the troops, in order that the passage of the defile may remain open.

Supposing that the army marches in two columns, the cavalry of the right will file by its left, the second line moving first, and taking the lead of the second column: the infantry of the second line, followed by the first, will place itself in the rear and follow this cavalry.

The cavalry of the left wing will file by its left, the second line moving first, and heading the first column. This will be joined by the infantry of the left wing, (whose second line will also move before the first), and thus the first column will be formed.

Six battalions of the rear of the first line, supported by ten squadrons of hussars: will form the rear guard. These six battalions are to place themselves in order of battle in front of the defile in two lines. Whilst the army is passing the defile, the troops that are posted in front must cover and protect by their fire those which still remain on the other side of it.

When the whole army shall have come up, the first line of the advanced guard is to throw itself into the defile, having passed through the intervals of the second line; and when it is gone on, the second line will follow in the same manner, under cover of the fire of those who are posted on the other side, who are to follow last, and will form the rear guard.

The most difficult of all manoeuvres is, that of passing a river during a retreat in presence of the enemy. On this subject I cannot quote a better example than our repassing the Elbe at Kolin in the retreat of 1744.

But as towns are not always in the neighbourhood of such situations, I will suppose that your only resource is in two bridges. In such a case a large entrenchment is to be thrown up which will include both the bridges, leaving a small opening at the head of each of them.

This being done, we are to send across the river several pieces of

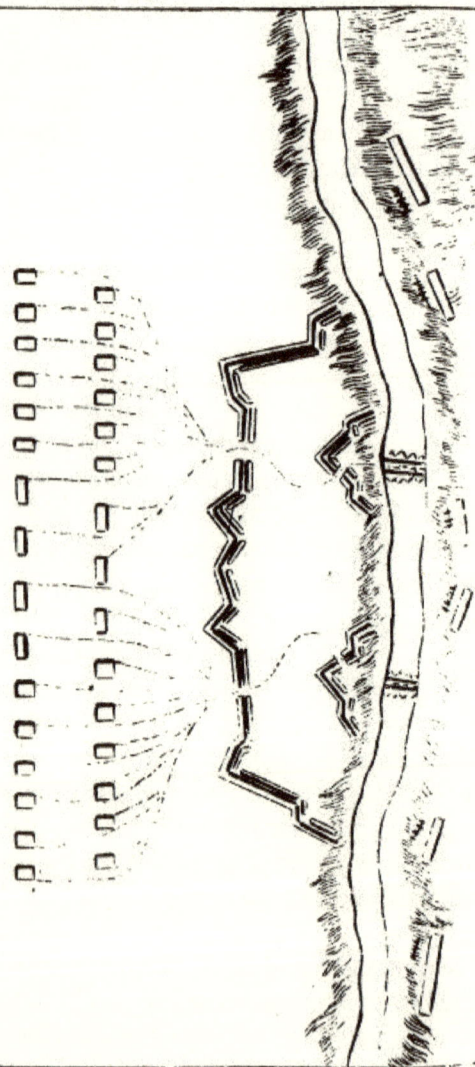

ADVANCE OF THE ARMY IN ENTRENCHMENTS passing a river. Lett. B.

cannon with a certain number of troops, and post them on the opposite bank, which should on no account be too steep, but sufficiently elevated to command that which is on the other side. The large entrenchment is then to be lined with infantry, and after such disposition, the infantry are to be the first to pass over, whilst the cavalry, forming the rear guard, retire in a chequered way through the entrenchment.

When all are passed, the two small heads of the bridge are to be skirted by infantry, whilst those who are in the entrenchment leave it, in order to retire.

If the enemy have any inclination for a pursuit, he will be exposed to the fire from both heads of the bridge, and from the troops who are posted on the other side of the river.

The infantry who were placed in the entrenchment having passed the river, the bridge is to be destroyed, and the troops who defended the heads of the bridge, are to pass over in boats, under cover of those who are posted on the other side of the river, whose duty it is to advance in order to support them.

When the pontoons are placed on the carriages, the last troops put themselves in motion.

Fougasses, (small mines fired on leaving entrenchments, rendering them useless to the enemy), may also be formed at the angles of the entrenchments, which may be set on fire by the last grenadiers at the moment that they have passed the riven

ARTICLE 16

On the Precautions necessary to be taken in a Retreat against Hussars and *Pandours*.

The hussars and *pandours*, (Hungarian foot soldiers), are dreadful only to those who do not know them. They are never brave but when animated by the hope of plunder, or when they can annoy others without exposing themselves. The first species of their bravery they exercise against convoys and baggage, and the other against troops who are obliged to retire, whom they endeavour to tease in their retreat.

Our troops have nothing serious to dread from them, but as a march is often retarded by their manner of skirmishing, and as some men will unavoidably be lost, and that too at a very inconvenient season, I shall explain the best method that I am acquainted with of getting rid of these gentry.

When we retreat through plains, the hussars are to be driven away by a few discharges of cannon, and the *pandours* by means of the dragoons and hussars of whom they are in a very great dread. The most difficult retreats, and those in which the *pandours* have it in their power to do the greatest mischief are those where we have to pass woods, defiles, and mountains. In such cases, the loss of some men is almost inevitable.

In these situations, then, the heights should be occupied, by the advanced guard with their front towards the enemy, and at the same time troops are to be detached on the flank of the line of march, who keeping along on the side of the army will always pass over the heights or through the woods. Some squadrons should also be at hand to be employed where the ground will allow of it.

On these occasions, we are never to halt, but keep constantly moving, for halting would certainly be an unseasonable sacrifice of some of your men.

The *pandours* fire as they lie down, and by that means keep themselves concealed; and when the marching of the army makes it necessary for the rear guard and the small parties that were detached to quit the heights and follow the main body, they then possess themselves of those situations, and being under cover, pick off those who are retreating. Neither musketry or cannon loaded with cartridge can do them much mischief, as they are scattered and concealed behind the heights and trees.

I made two retreats of this kind in the year 1745; one by the valley of Liebenthal, when marching to Staudenitz, and the other from Trautenau to Schatzlar. Notwithstanding every possible precaution, we lost sixty men *killed* and *wounded* in the first retreat, and more than two hundred in the second.

When we have to retreat through difficult ways, our marches should be very short, that we may be the more readily and perfectly on our guard. The longest march should not exceed two leagues, or one German mile, and as then we are not hurried, we are sometimes able to force the *pandours*, especially if they are imprudent enough to take shelter in a wood, which it is in our power to turn.

ARTICLE 17

Of the Method in which the Light Prussian Troops conduct themselves when engaged with the Hussars and *Pandours*.

Our plan in forcing a post which is occupied by the enemy's light troops is, to attack it hastily, for as they disperse in their mode of fighting, they cannot stand against the attack of our regular troops, who are never to mince the matter with them.

We have only to detach a few troops to cover the flanks of the party which marches against them, and then attack them with spirit, to insure their running away.

Our dragoons and hussars attack them closely formed and sword in hand, and as this is a sort of rencontre which they cannot endure, it has always happened that we have beaten, them, without paying any regard to the superiority of their numbers.

ARTICLE 18

By what Movements on our Side the Enemy may also be obliged to move

We are egregiously mistaking, if we suppose that the mere movement of an army will oblige the enemy also to put himself in motion. This is to be effected not simply by moving, but by the manner in which it is conducted. An intelligent enemy will not be induced to stir on account of any specious manoeuvres which you may think proper to practise: settled positions must be taken up that will oblige him to reflect, and reduce him to the necessity of decamping.

For this reason, we should be well informed of the nature of the country, the abilities of the general to whom we are opposed, the situation of his magazines, the towns that are most convenient to him, and those from which he draws his forage, and when these various circumstances are well combined together, the plan is to be formed and maturely digested.

That general who has the most fertile imagination, and attempts the most frequently to distress his enemy, will eventually rival his antagonist in glory.

He who at the opening of a campaign is the most alert in the assembling his troops, and marches forward to attack a town or occupy a post, will oblige his adversary to be regulated by his motions, and remain on the defensive.

You must always be possessed of very good reasons for wishing to oblige the enemy to move during a campaign: whether with a view of taking a town near which he is encamped, driving him to a barren country where he will hardly be able to exist, or with the hope of bringing on an engagement which will prove of material advantage. Induced by reasons of this nature, you set about arranging your plan, taking care that the marches which you are to make, and the camps which you are to occupy, do not lead you into greater inconveniencies than the enemy will suffer, by drawing you away from your depot,

Preussen.

Generalmajor v. Werner als Regimentschef   Husar.
in kleiner Uniform.

Husaren-Regiment v. Werner.
(1806 Husaren-Regiment Schimmelpfennig v. d. Oye No. 6.)
1758.

which may be in a place but badly fortified, and liable to be plundered by the light troops during your absence; by taking up a position where you may be cut off from all communication with your own country, or by occupying a situation which you will soon be obliged to abandon for want of subsistence.

After serious deliberation on these objects, and after having calculated the chances of enterprise on the part of the enemy, your plan is to be arranged, either for the purpose of encamping on one of his flanks, approaching the provinces whence he draws his subsistence, cutting him off from his *capitol*, threatening his depots, or, in short, taking up any position by which you deprive him of provisions.

To give an instance with which the greatest part of my officers are well acquainted I had formed a plan by which I had reason to hope that I should oblige Prince Charles of Lorraine to abandon Kônigingraetz and Pardubitz in the year 1745.

When we quitted the camp at Dubletz, we ought to have gone to the left, passed along by the county of Glatz, and inarched near Hohenmauth. By this manoeuvre we should have forced the Austrians, whose magazines were at Teutschbrod, and whose provisions were, for the most part, drawn from Moravia, to have marched to Landscron, leaving to us Kônigingraetz and Pardubitz. The Saxons, being cut off from their home, would have been obliged to quit the Austrians, in order to cover their own country.

What prevented my making this manoeuvre at that period was, that I should have profited nothing if I had gained Kônigingraetz, as I must have sent detachments to the support of the Prince of Anhalt, in case that the Saxons had returned home. Besides this circumstance, the magazines at Glatz were not equal to the subsistence of my army during the whole of the campaign.

The diversions that are made by detaching troops, will also sometimes oblige the enemy to decamp, for generally speaking, every kind of enterprise that comes on him unawares will have the effect of deranging him, and obliging him to quit his position.

Of such nature are the passing of mountains which the enemy deems impassable, and the crossing of rivers without his knowledge.

Sufficient information is to be gained on this head by reading the campaign of Prince Eugene in the year 1701. The confusion of the French Army when it was surprised by Prince Charles of Lorraine, who had crossed the Rhine, is a matter sufficiently well understood.

I shall conclude by saying, that the execution of enterprises of this nature should always correspond with the design, and as long as the general's dispositions are wise and founded on solid principles, so long will he have it in his power to give the law to his enemy, and oblige him to keep on the defensive..

ARTICLE 19

Of the Crossing of Rivers

As long as the enemy remains on the other side of a river which you wish to cross, all force is useless, and recourse must be made to stratagem. To be informed how we are to pass a large river, we have only to consult Caesar's passage of the Rhine, that of the Po by Prince Eugene, or of the Rhine by Prince Charles of Lorraine.

These generals sent out detachments to impose upon the enemy, and conceal the spot where they intended to pass. They made every preparation for the building of bridges in places where they had no idea of employing them whilst the main body of the army, by a night march, gained a considerable distance from the enemy, and had time to pass the river before the troops, who were to dispute their passage, could be put in order to prevent them.

We generally choose to cross rivers at those parts where there are some small islands, as they forward the business very materially. We wish also to meet on the other side with woods or other obstacles, that may prevent the enemy from attacking us before we have had time to get into proper order.

The most prudent measures and the most particular attention are required in enterprises of this nature. The boats or pontoons with every other article of necessary apparatus must be at the *rendezvous* by the appointed hour, and every boatman well instructed what he has to do, to avoid the confusion which generally attends expeditions by night. Everything being arranged, the troops are to pass over and establish themselves on the other side of the river.

Whenever rivers are to be crossed, care should be taken that the two heads of the bridge be entrenched, and well furnished with troops. The islands which are in the neighbourhood should be fortified, in order to support the entrenchments, and prevent the enemy, daring your operations, from seizing or destroying the bridges

If the rivers be narrow, we choosy our passage at those parts where they form angles, and where the bank, by being a little more elevated, commands that on the opposite side.

On this spot we place as many cannon, with a proportionate number of troops, as the ground will allow, under the protection of which the bridges are to be built; and as the ground grows narrower on account of the angle, we are to advance but very little, and insensibly gain ground as the troops pass.

If there be any fords, we slope the ground leading to them, to enable the cavalry to pass.

ARTICLE 20
Of the Manner in which the Passage of Rivers is to be defended.

Nothing is more difficult, not to say impossible, than to defend the passage of a river, especially when the front of attack be of too great an extent. I would never undertake a commission of this kind, if the ground which I had to defend was more than eight German miles in front, and unless there were two or three redoubts established on the bank of the river within this distance; neither should any other part of the river be fordable.

But supposing the situation to be exactly as I have stated, time must always be required to make the necessary preparations against the enterprises of the enemy, the disposition of which should be nearly as follows:—

All the boats and barks which can be found upon the river should be got together, and conveyed to the two redoubts, that the enemy may not have it in his power to make use of them.

Both the banks of the river are to be reconnoitred, that you may discover and destroy those parts of them where it would be possible to pass.

The ground which might protect the passage of the enemy is to be particularly attended to, and your plans of attack must be regulated by the nature and situation of each part of it.

Roads sufficiently wide to admit of many columns are to be made along the whole front of the river which you are to defend, that you may march against the enemy free of every impediment.

These precautions being taken, the army is to be encamped in the centre of the line of defence, that you may have but four miles to march to either extremity.

Sixteen small detachments are then to be formed, and commanded by the most active, intelligent officers of dragoons and hussars; eight of which, under the orders of a general officer, are to have charge of the front of attack on the right, whilst the other eight, commanded in like manner, take care of the left.

These detachments will be designed to give information of the de-my's movements, and of the spot where it will be his intention to pass.

During the day, guards are to be posted to discover what is going forward, and by night patrols are to go out every quarter of an hour near to the river, and not retire till they have distinctly seen that the enemy has made a bridge, and that the head has passed.

The aforesaid generals and commanding officers of redoubts are to send their reports to the commander in chief four times a day.

Fresh horses should be stationed between them and the army, in order to hasten the arrival of their dispatches, and inform the general as immediately as possible when the enemy is about to pass. As it is the duty of the general to repair thither at a moment's warning, his baggage should be sent away beforehand, that he may be ready for every event.

The different dispositions for each part of the ground being already made, the generals are appointed by the commander in chief to those which regard the points of attack. No time is to be lost in marching, (the infantry taking the lead of the columns,) as you are to suppose that the enemy are entrenching themselves. When arrived, the attack is to be made instantly and with great spirit, as the only means of promising to yourself brilliant success.

The passages of small rivers are still more difficult to defend; their fords are to be rendered impassable, if possible, by throwing in of trees. But if the enemy's bank commands yours it is vain to attempt resistance.

Article 21

Of the Surprise of Towns

A town must be badly guarded and weakly fortified that suffers a surprise; and if it's ditches be filled with water, the success of such enterprise must depend on a wintry season and hard frost.

Towns may be surprised by a whole army, as was the case at Prague in the year 1741, or the accident may happen from the garrison having been lulled into security by a long continued blockade, as was effected by Prince Leopold d'Anhalt at Glogau. Detachments also sometimes have the desired effect, as was attempted by Prince Eugene at Cremona, and as succeeded with the Austrians at Cosel.

The principal rule in making dispositions for surprises is, to be well informed of the nature of the fortifications and of the interiors of the place, so as to direct your attack to any particular spot.

The surprise of Glogau was a *chef d'œuvre*, and is well worth the imitation of those who attempt such enterprises. There was nothing so extraordinary in the surprise of Prague, as it was impossible but such a variety of attacks must carry a place, where the garrison had so great an extent to defend. Cosel and Cremona were betrayed; the first by an officer who deserted and informed the Austrians that the excavation of the ditch was not quite completed, by which means they got over, and the place was carried.

If we wish to take small places, we batter some of the gates with mortars, whilst detachments are sent to the others to prevent the garrison from saving themselves.

If cannon are to be employed, they must be so placed that the artillerymen be not exposed to the fire of the musquetry; otherwise the guns will be in danger of being lost.

ARTICLE 22
Of Combats and Battles.

The Austrian camp is surrounded by such a number of light troops, as to render a surprise a work of very great difficulty.

If two armies keep near to each other, the business will very soon be decided, unless one of them occupies an inaccessible post that will secure it from surprises; a circumstance which seldom takes place between armies, though it be nothing uncommon between detachments.

To have it in our power to surprise an enemy in his camp, it is necessary that he never expects such event, and that he relies entirely either on the superiority of his troops, the advantageous situation of his post, the reports of his emissaries, or lastly, on the vigilance of his light troops.

The nature of the country and the position of the enemy should be perfectly well understood prior to the formation of any plan.

The roads leading to camp must be well examined, and the general disposition of things formed from thence, being regulated in every point by the particular and exact knowledge of all attendant circumstances.

The most intelligent *chasseurs*, who are best acquainted with the roads, should be appointed to conduct the columns.

Be particularly careful to conceal your design, for secrecy is the soul of all enterprises.

The light troops should take the lead on the march, for which regulation various reasons may be assigned, though the real one be to prevent any scoundrel of a deserter from betraying you. They will also be of service by preventing the enemy's patrols from approaching too nearly and discovering your movements.

The generals who are under your orders must be well instructed of all events that may happen, and how to act when any accident occurs.

If the enemy's camp be situate in a plain, an advanced guard may be formed of dragoons, who, being joined by the hussars, will enter the enemy's camp on full speedy throw it into contusion, and cut down whatever comes in their way.

The whole army should support these dragoons, and the infantry being at the head of it, should be particularly employed in attacking the wings of the enemy's cavalry.

The advanced guard should begin the attack half an hour before day, but the army should not be more than eight hundred yards in it's rear.

During the march the most profound silence is to be observed, and the soldiers must be forbidden to smoke tobacco.

When the attack has commenced and the day appears, the infantry, formed into four or six columns, must march strait forward to the camp, in order to support its advanced guard.

No firing is to be allowed before daylight as it might prove the means of destroying our own people: but as soon as the day is broke, we should fire on all those places into which the advanced guard has not penetrated, especially on the wings of the cavalry, that we may oblige the troopers, who have not time to accoutre their horses, to abandon them and fly.

The enemy are to be followed even out of their camp, and the whole of the cavalry should be let loose after them to take advantage of their disorder and confusion.

If the enemy have abandoned their arms, a strong detachment must be left in charge of the camp, whilst the remainder of the army, instead of amusing themselves with plunder, pursue the enemy with all possible ardour; the more so, as a like opportunity of entirely routing them, may not soon present itself, and we may, by so doing, have the upper hand during the whole campaign, and be able to act just as we think proper.

Fortune intended to favour me with an opportunity of this kind before the Battle of Mollwitz: we approached the army of the Marshal de Neuperg without being perceived, as they were cantoned in three villages: but at that time I wanted information how to profit by such circumstance.

My business then was, to have surrounded the village of Mollwitz by two columns, and to have attacked it. At the same moment I should have detached some dragoons to the other two villages where the Austrian cavalry lay, in order to throw them into confusion, whilst the infantry who followed them would have prevented the cavalry from mounting. By this method I am persuaded that the whole army would have been destroyed.

I have already shewn the necessary cautions that respect our camp, and the manner in which it is to be protected: but if in spite of all our care, the enemy should approach the army, I would advise that the troops be formed in order of battle on the ground which is allotted to them, and that the cavalry remain firm on their posts, firing by platoons till daybreak. The generals are then to examine whether it be advisable to advance, if the cavalry has been victorious or suffered a repulse, and what farther methods are to be pursued.

On such occasions, each general should know how to act *independently*, without being obliged to wait for the instructions of the commander in chief.

For my own part, I am determined never to attack by night, on account of the confusion which darkness necessarily occasions, and because the major part of the soldiery require the eye of their officers, and the fear of punishment, to induce them to do their duty.

Charles XII. in the year 1715, attacked the Prince of Anhalt in the night, though he was but just disembarked on the island of Rugen. The King of Sweden had reason for so doing, as daylight would have discovered the weakness of his army. He came with four thousand men to attack five times the number, and of course was defeated.

It is an invariable axiom of war, to secure your own flanks and rear, and endeavour to turn those of your enemy. This may be done in different ways, though they all depend on the same principle.

When you are obliged to attack an entrenched enemy, it should be done instantly, without allowing him time to finish his works. What would be of advantage *today*, may not be so *tomorrow*.

But before you set about making the attack, the enemy's position must be well reconnoitred with your own eyes, and your first dispositions of attack will convince you whether your scheme will be easily put into execution, or become a work of labour and difficulty.

The want of sufficient support is the chief reason that entrenchments are taken. The entrenchment of Turenne was carried, as was also

Preußen. Kleistsches Freikorps: Ungarisches Infanterie=Regiment. 1763.

Unteroffizier   Tambour   Offizier

that of ————. (probably that of Schellenberg), because there was sufficient ground to enable the Prince of Anhalt to turn it. That of Malplaquet was turned by the wood which was on the Marshal Villars' left. Had the allies been aware of this circumstance at the beginning of the battle, it would have saved their army fifteen thousand men.

If a fordable river support the entrenchment, it must be attacked on that side. The work at Stralsund, conducted by the Swedes, was carried because the attack was made on the sea-side, where it happened to be fordable.

If the enemy's entrenchments are of too great an extent, so that the troops are obliged to occupy more ground than they can well defend, we attack at several points, and provided we can keep our designs secret from the enemy, (which will prevent his meeting us with a sufficient force), we shall certainly get possession of the works.

I will explain the following dispositions of an attack on an entrenchment, where I shall form the line with thirty battalions, and strengthen the left wing by the river N. N. The attack on the left, where I wish to penetrate, shall be made by twelve battalions, and that on the right by eight. The troops destined for the attack are to be formed in a chequered way, with the allowance of proper intervals. The remainder of the infantry are to throw themselves into the third line, and behind them, at the distance of four hundred yards, the cavalry should be posted. By this means my infantry will keep the enemy in check, and be ready to take advantage of any false movement which he may make.

Care must be taken that each of these attacks be followed closely by a number, of pioneers with shovels, pick-axes, and fascines to fill up the ditch, and make a road for the cavalry, when the entrenchment shall have been forced.

The infantry who form the attack are not to fire till the work be carried, and they are drawn up in order of battle on the parapet.

The cavalry are to enter through the openings made by the pioneers, and attack the enemy as soon as they find themselves of sufficient force. If the cavalry be repulsed, they must rally under cover of the infantry's fire until the whole army has got in, and the enemy are entirely routed.

I must here repeat, that I would never entrench my army unless I had a siege in contemplation; and I am not decided, whether it be not the best plan to go on before the army that comes to relieve a place.

But supposing for a moment, that we have an inclination to entrench ourselves; to execute such intention, the following method appears to me the most advantageous.

We contrive to have two or three large reserves, which are to be sent out during the attack to those points where the enemy is making his greatest efforts.

The parapet is to he lined by battalions, and a reserve placed behind them, to be at hand in case of necessity. The cavalry should be ranged in one line behind these reserves.

The entrenchment should be very well supported, and if it be joined by a river, the ditch should be carried some distance info it, to prevent it's being turned.

If it be strengthened by a wood, it should be closed at that end by a redoubt, and a large abbatis of trees should also be made in the wood.

Particular regard must be paid to the flanking of the redans.

The ditch should be very deep and wide, and the entrenchments must be improved every day, either by strengthening the parapet, placing *pallisadoes* at the entrance of the barriers, digging of pits, or furnishing the whole of the camp with *chevaux de frize*.

The greatest advantage you have is, in the choice of your work, and in the observance of certain rules of fortification which will oblige the enemy to attack you on a small front, and that only in the principle points of your entrenchment,

The plate opposite will give you a more exact idea of this business. The army, which is there placed at the head of the entrenchment, is thrown back on one side by the river, so that you present a projecting front to the enemy who comes to attack you. Your right is safe from attack by means of the batteries placed at the extremities of that wing, which would play upon the enemy's flank, whilst the centre redoubt would take him in the rear. The only point liable to attack therefore is the centre redoubt) and even here he will be obliged to cut his way through the abbatis.

In your preparations for this attack it behoves you therefore to strengthen the fortifications of this redoubt, and as you have but one point which demands your particular attention, that one will consequently be more perfect and complete.

The second plate over the page, exhibits entrenchments of a different kind, which are composed of projecting and receding redoubts, which cross each other, and are connected by entrenchments.

By this method of fortification, those that project form the points of attack, and as they are but few of them, much less time is required

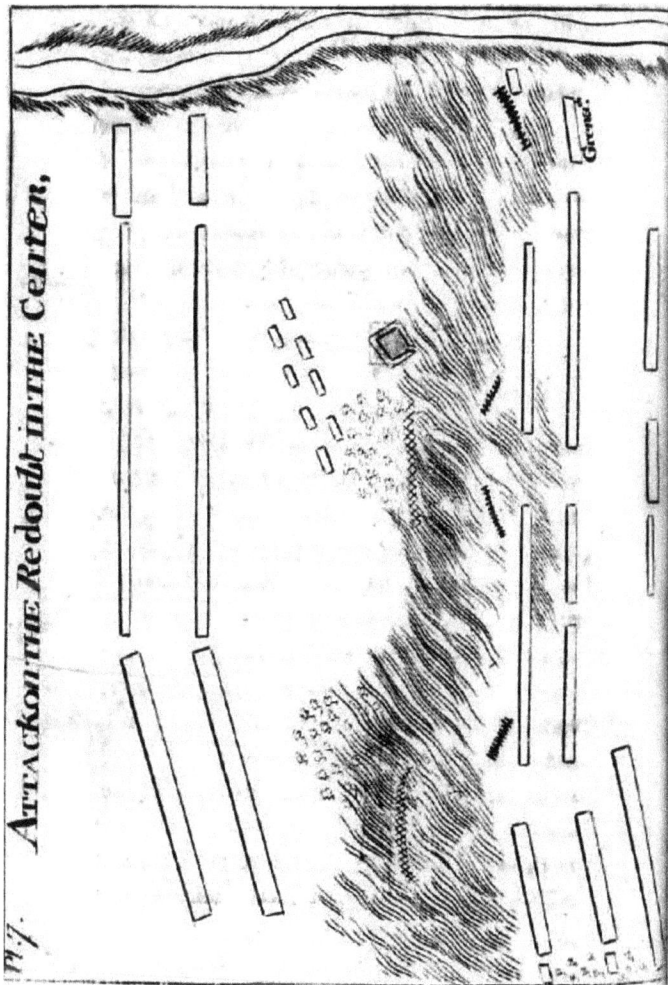

Pl. 7.   ATTACK on the Redoubt in the Center.

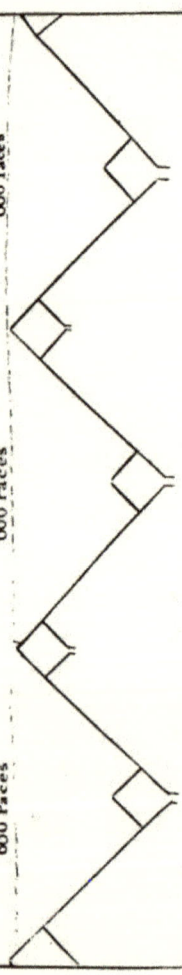

Intrenchment compofed of
Counter Salient Redoubts.

600 Paces

600 Paces

600 Paces

600 Paces

in completing them, than if the whole front was to be equally well fortified.

In these projecting redoubts, the fire of the musquetry must always cross each other, and for this reason they should never be more than six hundred yards apart.

Our infantry defend an entrenchment by the fire of entire battalions, and every soldier should be provided with one hundred rounds. This, however, is not to prevent the placing as many cannon as we can between the battalions and the projecting redoubts.

Whilst the enemy are at a distance, we fire shot, but when they approach within four hundred yards, we have recourse to cartridges.

If, notwithstanding the strength of your entrenchment, and the smartness of your fire, the enemy should make any impression, the reserve of infantry must march forward to repel him, and if they also be obliged to fall back, your last effort to put him to the route must depend upon your cavalry.

The principal reasons why entrenchments are carried are these, the want of attention to proper rules in their construction, or the troops being turned or panic struck: the superior freedom and boldness with which the attackers are able to conduct themselves, gives them this advantage.

Examples have already shewn, that when an entrenchment is forced, the whole army is discouraged and put to flight: I have a better opinion of my troops, and am persuaded that they would repel the enemy; but what end would this answer, if the entrenchments prevent their profiting by such advantages?

As there are so many inconveniencies attending entrenchments, it naturally follows that lines are still more useless. The fashion of our day is that which was practised by Prince Louis de Baden, whose first lines were made on the side of Briel. The French also employed them after that in Flanders. I maintain that they are of no service whatever, since they compass more ground than the troops can possibly defend; they allow of a variety of attacks being made on them, and tempt the enemy to force a passage. On this account they do not cover the country, but, on the contrary, ensure the loss of reputation to the troops who have to defend them.

Although a Prussian Army should be inferior to that which is opposed to them, they are not to despair of success, as the general's *management* will supply the want of numbers.

An army that is weak should always make choice of a difficult, mountainous country, where the ground narrows, so that the superior number of the enemy, not being able to pass their wings, becomes useless, and often an encumbrance to them.

It may here be added, that in a country which is close and hilly, the wings can better be supported than when we are on a plain. We should not have gained the Battle of Sohr but for the advantage of the ground, for though the Austrian Army doubled ours, they were not able to break through our wings, as the ground rendered both the armies nearly equal.

The choice of ground is my first object, and my second the disposition of the battle itself; it is here that my oblique order of battle may be employed to advantage, for you refuse one wing to the enemy, whilst you strengthen that which ought to make the attack. By this means you turn all your force on that wing of the enemy which you wish to take in flank.

An army of ten thousand men, if its flanks are turned, will very soon be defeated, as may be seen by the plate opposite. Everything is done by my right wing. A body of infantry will move by degrees into the wood, to attack the flanks of the enemy's cavalry, and protect the onset of our own: some regiments of hussars should be ordered to take the enemy in the rear whilst the army advances, and when their cavalry are routed, the infantry who are in the wood must take the enemy's infantry in flank, whilst the remainder are attacking them in front.

My left wing will not stir till the enemy's left wing is entirely defeated.

By this disposition you will gain the following advantages: 1st, that of making head with a small force against a much superior number; 2ndly, of attacking the enemy at a point which will decide the business; 3rdly, if your wing should chance to be beaten, as only a small part of your army has been engaged, three fourths of your troops, who are fresh, will be ready to support you in your retreat.

If you wish to attack an enemy that is advantageously posted, you must carefully examine both his strong and his weak side before you make your dispositions for attack, and always choose that point where you expect to meet with the least resistance.

So many men are lost in the attacks on villages, that I have vowed never to undertake them, unless obliged by absolute necessity, for you run the hazard of losing the flower of your infantry.

It is said by some generals, that the most proper point of attack is

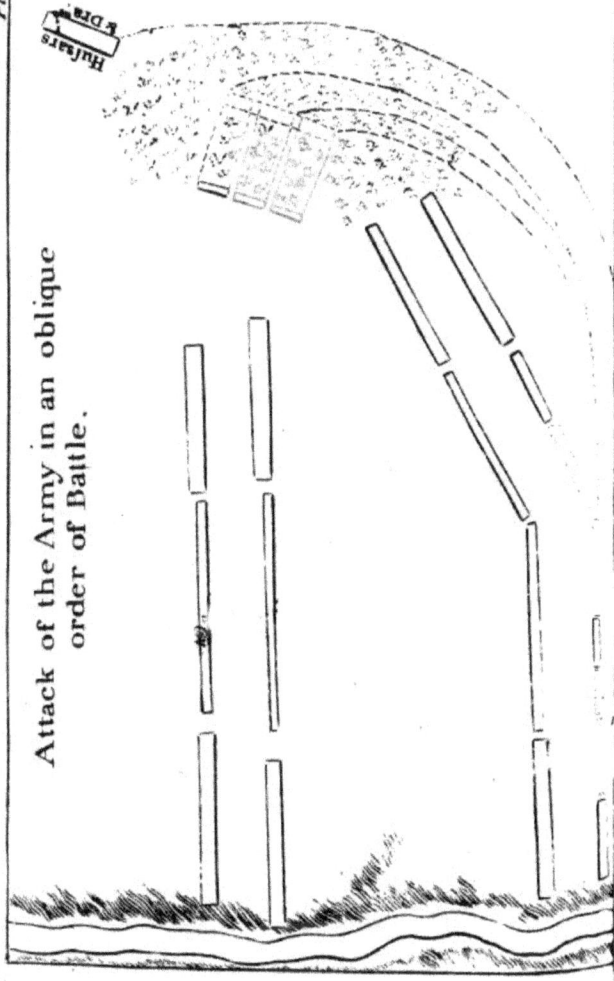

Attack of the Army in an oblique order of Battle.

Hussars & Dra.

Pl. 9.

the centre of a post. The plate opposite will represent the situation of such a post, where I suppose the enemy to have two large towns and two villages on its wings. The wings must certainly be lost, when you have forced the centre, and by similar attacks, the most complete victories may be obtained.

It must be added to the plan which I here lay down, that you must double your attack when you have once made an impression, in order to force the enemy to fall back both on his right hand and upon his left.

Nothing is so formidable in the attack of a post, as the discharge of cartridges from the batteries, which made a terrible havoc amongst the battalions. I witnessed the attacks on the batteries of Sohr and Kesselsdorf, and shall here communicate the idea suggested by my reflections on that business, supposing that we wish to be possessed of a battery mounted with fifteen pieces of cannon, which it is not in our power to turn.

I have remarked, that the fire of cannon and of the infantry who defend a battery render it inaccessible. We cannot make ourselves masters of the enemy's batteries but through their own fault: finding our infantry who attacked half destroyed and giving way, the infantry of the enemy quit their post to follow them, and being by this movement deprived of the use of their cannon, when they return to their batteries, our people enter with them and take possession.

The experience of those two battles gave me the idea, that in similar cases we should copy the example of our troops on this occasion, *viz.* to form the attack in two lines in a chequered way, and to be supported in the third line by some squadrons of dragoons.

The first line should be ordered to attack but faintly, and fall back through the intervals of the second, so that the enemy, deceived by this sham retreat, may abandon his post in order to pursue us.

This movement of theirs is to be our signal to advance and make a vigorous attack.

The disposition of this manoeuvre is explained in the plate over the page.

It is my principle, never to place my whole confidence in one post, unless it can be physically proved to be safe from any attack.

The great dependence of our troops is in attacking, and we should act a very foolish part to give up this point without good reason.

But if it be necessary that posts should be occupied, we remember to get possession of the sights, and make our wings sufficiently strong.

Pl. 10.

Attack of the army on the Center

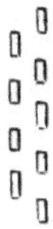

Oebeße

SCHATZLAR

Wisthausen

Brandewate

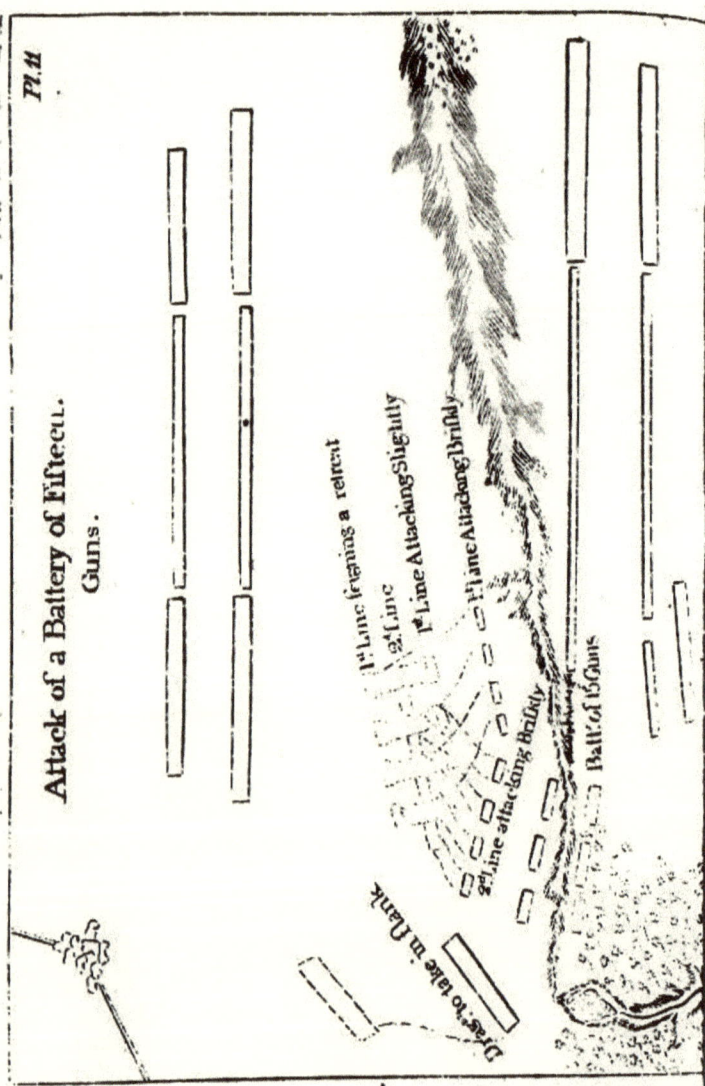

Pl. 44

Attack of a Battery of Fifteen Guns.

1st Line forming a retreat
2d Line
1st Line Attacking Slightly
1st Line Attacking Briskly
2d Line attacking Briskly
Batt of 15 Guns
Direc to take in flank

I would burn every village which is at the head or on the wings of the army, if the wind did not drive the smoke into the camp.

If there were any strong *stone* houses in front, I would defend them by the infantry, in order to annoy the enemy during the action.

Great care should be taken, not to place troops on ground where they cannot act; it was *this* which made our position at Grotkau in the year 1741 worth nothing, for the centre and left wing were posted behind impassable bogs. The only ground that would admit of being manoeuvred on, was that which was occupied by a part of the right wing.

Villeroy was beaten at Ramillies for the very reason that I have just mentioned, as his right wing was rendered entirely useless, and the enemy crowded all its force against the right wing of the French, which could make no resistance.

I allow the Prussian troops to take possession of advantageous posts as well as other troops, and to make use of them in favour of any movement, or to take advantage of their artillery; but they must quit this post instantly to march against the enemy, who, instead of being allowed to begin the attack, is attacked himself, and sees all his projects miscarry. Every movement which we make in presence of the enemy without his expecting it, will certainly produce a good effect.

We must rank battles of this kind amongst the best, always remembering to attack the weakest point.

On these occasions, I would not permit the infantry to fire, for it only retards their march, and the victory is not decided by the number of slain, but by the extent of territory which you have gained.

The most certain way of insuring victory is, to march briskly and in good order against the enemy, always endeavouring to gain ground.

It is the custom to allow fifteen, yards of interval between squadrons in a difficult, intersected country, but where the ground is good and even, they form in a line entire.

No greater interval is to be allowed between the infantry than is sufficient for the cannon. It is only in attacks of entrenchments, batteries, and villages, and in the formation of the rear guard in a retreat, that the cavalry and infantry are placed in a chequered way, in order to give an immediate support to the first line by making the second fall into its intervals, so that the troops may retire without disorder, and be a mutual support to each other. This is a rule never to be neglected.

An opportunity offers itself here of giving you some principal rules on what you are to observe when you range the army in order of battle, whatever the ground may happen to be. The first is, to take up points of view for the wings; the right wing, for example, will align itself by the steeple N. N.

The general must be particularly careful that he does not suffer the troops to take up a wrong position.

It is not always necessary to defer the attack till the whole army can engage, as opportunity may present advantages which would be lost by a little delay.

A *great* part of the army, however, ought to be engaged, and the first line should be the chief object in the regulation of the order of battle. If all the regiments of that line are not present, they should be replaced by the same number of the second.

The wings should always be well-supported, especially those which are expected to make the greatest exertions.

In an open country, the order of battle should be equally strong throughout, for as the enemy's movements are unconfined, he may have reserved a part of his army which he may make use of to cut you out a little employment.

In case that one of the two wings should not be properly supported, the general who commands the second line should send some dragoons thither, (without waiting for an order on the occasion) to extend the first line, and the hussars taken from the third line should replace the dragoons.

The reason for so doing is, that if the enemy makes a movement to take the cavalry of the first line in flank, your dragoons and hussars may be able in their turn to repay the compliment.

You will see in the following plate that I place three battalions in the interval between the two lines of the left wing, the better to support it: for supposing your cavalry to be beaten, these battalions will always prevent the enemy from falling foul on the infantry, an instance of which we witnessed at Mollwitz.

The general commanding the second line must preserve a distance of three hundred paces from the first, and if he perceive any intervals in the first line, he is to fill them up with battalions from the second.

In a plain, a reserve of cavalry should always be placed in the rear of the centre of the battalions, and be commanded by an officer of address, as he is to act from himself, either in support of a wing that he sees hardly pressed, or by flanking the enemy who are in pursuit of the wing that is thrown into disorder, that the cavalry may in the meantime have an opportunity of rallying.

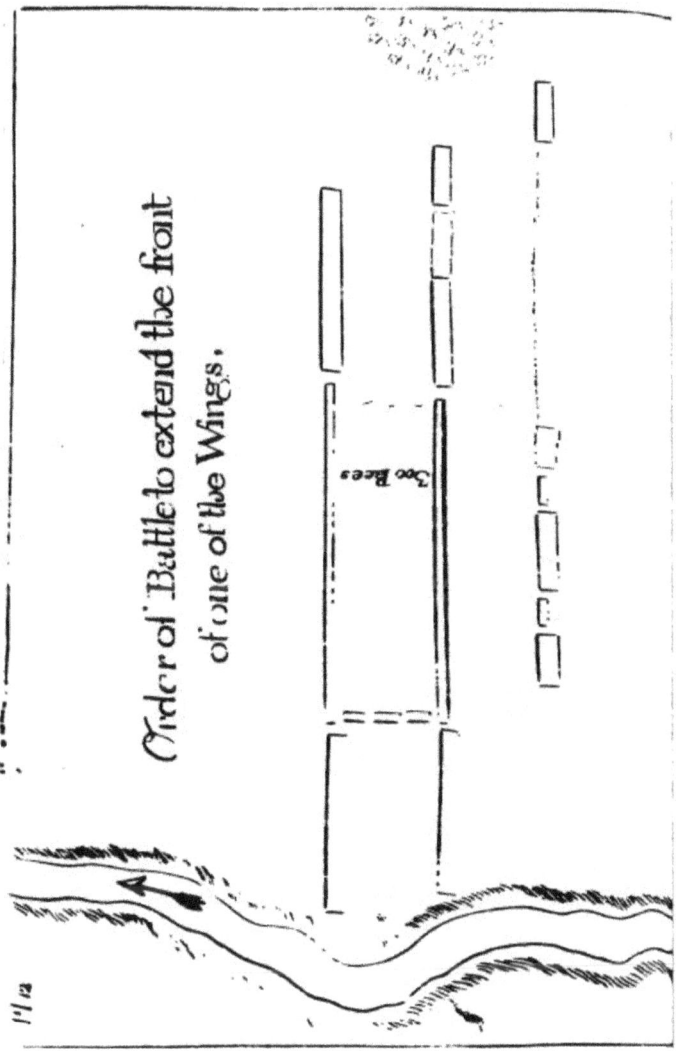

Order of Battle to extend the front of one of the Wings.

300 Paces

The affair should be begun by the cavalry on full gallop, and the infantry also should march on briskly towards the enemy. Commanding officers are to take care that their troops penetrate and entirely break through the enemy, and that they make no use of their fire arms till their backs are turned.

If the soldiers fire without the word of command, they are to be ordered to *shoulder arms*, and proceed without any halting.

When the enemy begins to give way, we fire, by battalions, and a battle conducted in this manner will very soon be decided.

A new order of battle is represented in the plate opposite, which differs from the others in having bodies of infantry placed at the extremities of the wings of the cavalry. The battalions are intended to support the cavalry, by playing with their own cannon and those belonging to the wings of the cavalry, on the enemy's cavalry at the beginning of the affair, that our own may have a better game to play during the attack. Another reason is, that supposing your wing to be beaten, the enemy dare not pursue, for fear of being between two fires.

When your cavalry, to all appearance, has been victorious, this infantry is to approach that of the enemy, and the battalions which are in the intervals must make a quarter-wheel and place themselves on your wings, to take the enemy's infantry in flank and rear, and enable you to make a handsome business of it.

The conquering wing of your cavalry must not allow the enemy's cavalry to rally, but pursue them in good order, and endeavour to cut them off from the infantry. When the confusion becomes general, the commanding officer should detach the hussars after them, who are to be supported by the cavalry. At the same time some dragoons should be sent to the roads which the infantry have taken, in order to pick them up, and by cutting off their retreat, make a great number of them prisoners.

There is another difference in this order of battle, which is, that the squadrons of dragoons are mixed with the infantry of the second line: this is done, because I have remarked in all the affairs which we have had with the Austrians, that after the fire of their musquetry has continued for about a quarter. of an hour, they get together round their colours; at Hohen Friedberg our cavalry charged many of these *round-about* parties, and made a great number of them prisoners. The dragoons, being near at hand, are to be let loose instantly, and they never fail to give a very good account of them.

It will be said, that I never employ my small arms, but that it is my

New Order of Battle

Drag. Drag. Drag. Drag.

Cavalry

wish in all these dispositions to make use of my artillery only: to this I answer, that one of the two accidents which I suppose will unavoidably happen, either that my infantry fire in spite of my orders to the contrary, or that they obey my commands, and the enemy begins to give way. In either case, as soon as you perceive any confusion amongst their troops, you are to detach the cavalry after them, and when they find themselves attacked in flank on one side, charged in front, and their second line of cavalry cut off by the rear, the greatest part of them will be sure to fall into your hands.

It then cannot be called a battle, but an entire destruction of your enemies, especially if there be no defile in the neighbourhood to protect their flights

I shall close this article with a single reflection, *viz.* if you march to battle in column, whether by the right or by the left, the battalions or divisions must follow each other closely, that when you begin to deploy, you may have it in your power readily to engage. But if you march in front, the distances of the battalions must be well attended to, that they be not too close or too far from each other.

I make a distinction between the heavy cannon and the field pieces attached to the battalions, as the former should be planted o the heights, and the latter fifty paces in front of the battalions. Both the one and the other should be well pointed and well fired.

When we are within five hundred yards of the enemy, the field pieces should be drawn by men, that they may fire without intermission as we advance.

If the enemy begin to fly, the heavy cannon are to move forward and fire a few rounds, by way of wishing them a good journey.

Six gunners and three regimental carpenters should be attached to every piece in the first line.

I had omitted saying, that at the distance of three hundred and fifty yards, the cannon should begin to fire cartridges.

But to what end serves the art of conquest, if we are ignorant how to profit by our advantage? To shed the blood of soldiers when there is no occasion for it, is to lead them inhumanly to the slaughter; and not to pursue the enemy on certain occasions, to increase their fear and the number of our prisoners, is leaving an affair to future chance which might be determined at the present moment. Nevertheless, you may sometimes be prevented from pursuing your conquest by a want of provisions, or the troops being too much fatigued.

It is always the fault of the general in chief if an army want provisions. When he gives battle, he has a design in so doing: and if he has a design, it is his duty to be provided with everything necessary for the execution of it, and of course he ought to be supplied with bread or biscuit for eight or ten days.

With respect to fatigues, if they had not been too excessive, they must not be regarded, as on extraordinary occasions extraordinary feats should be performed.

When victory is perfectly decided, I would recommend a detachment to be made of those regiments who have been the greatest sufferers, to take care of the wounded, and convey them to the hospitals, which ought to he already established. Though our own wounded are to be the first objects of our attention, we are not to forget our duty to the enemy.

In the meantime the army is to pursue the enemy to the nearest defile, which in the first transport of their alarm they will not tarry to keep possession of, if you take care not to allow them sufficient, time to recover their wind.

When you have attended to all these circumstances, the camp is to be marked out, paying strict regard to the established rules, and not allowing yourself to be lulled with too great an idea of security.

If the victory has been complete, we may send out detachments either to cut off the enemy's retreat, seize his magazines, or lay siege to three or four towns at the same time.

On this article, general rules only can be given, as a great deal must depend on fortuitous circumstances. You are never to imagine that everything is done as long as *any* thing remains undone; nor are you to suppose but that a cunning enemy, though he may have been beaten, will keep a sharp lookout to take advantage of your negligence or errors.

I pray to heaven, that the Prussians never way be beaten, and dare affirm that such an accident never will happen if they are well led on and well disciplined.

But should they meet with a disaster of such a nature, the following rules are to be observed in order to recover the misfortune. When you see that the battle is inevitably lost, and that it is not in your power to oppose the enemy's movements, or even resist them much longer, you are to send the second line of infantry to any defile that may be near, and place them in it agreeably to the disposition which I have given under the article of *retreats*, sending thither at the same time as many cannon as you can spare.

Vic—Aug. No 8.
Seydlitz Regiment

If there be no defile in the neighbourhood, the first line must retire through the interval of the second, and place itself in order of battle three hundred yards behind them.

All the remains of your cavalry must be got together, and if you choose it, they may be formed into a *square* to protect your retreat.

History furnishes us with accounts of two remarkable squares: one that was formed by General Schullembourg after the Battle of Frauenstadt, by means of which he retired across the Oder without being forced by Charles XII.; the other by the Prince of Anhalt when General Stirum lost the first Battle of Hochstaedt. This prince traversed a plain of two leagues, and the French cavalry did not dare to molest him.

I shall conclude with saying, that though we are defeated, there is no occasion for running away forty leagues, but that we are to halt at the first advantageous post, and put a bold face upon the business in order to collect the scattered army, and encourage those who are dispirited.

ARTICLE 23
Of the Reasons which should induce us to give Battle, and in what Manner it is to be conducted

Battles determine the fate of nations. It is necessary that actions should be decisive, either to free ourselves from the inconveniencies of a state of warfare, to place our enemy in that unpleasant situation, or to settle a quarrel which otherwise perhaps would never be finished. A man that is wise will make no sort of movement without good reason; and a general of an army should never be engaged without some design of consequence. If he be forced into an engagement by his adversary, his former errors must have reduced him to that situation, and given his enemy the power of dictating the law to him,

On the present occasion it will be seen, that I am not writing my own panegyric: for out of five battles which my troops have given to the enemy, three of them only were premeditated, and I was forced by the enemy into the other two. At the affair of Mollwitz the Austrians had posted themselves between my army and Wohlau, where I kept my provisions and artillery. At that of Sohr, the enemy had cut me off from the road to Trautenau, so that I was obliged to fight, or run the risk of losing my whole army. But how great is the difference between forced and premeditated battles! How brilliant was our success at Hohen-Friedberg, at Kesselsdorf, and also at Czaslau, which last engagement was the means of procuring us peace!

Though I am here laying down rules for battles, I do not pretend to deny that I have often erred through inadvertence; my officers, however, are expected to profit by my mistakes, and they may be assured, that I shall apply myself with all diligence to correct them.

It sometimes happens that both the armies wish to engage, and then the business is very soon settled.

Those battles are the best into which we force the enemy, for it is an established maxim, to oblige him to do that for which he has no sort of inclination, and as your interest and his are so diametrically opposite, it cannot be supposed that you are both wishing for the same event.

Many are the reasons that may induce us to give battle, such as, a desire to oblige the enemy to raise the siege of any place that may prove of convenience to yourself, to drive him out of a province which he possess, penetrate his country, enable yourself to lay a siege, correct him for his stubbornness if he refuse to make peace, or make him suffer for some error that he has committed.

You will also oblige the enemy to come to action when, by a forced march, you fall upon his rear and cut off his communications, or by threatening a town which it is his interest to preserve.

But in this sort of manoeuvre great care is to be taken that you do not get into the same embarrassed situation, or take up a position which enables the enemy to. cut you off from your magazines.

The affairs which are undertaken against rear guards are attended with the least danger.

If you entertain a design of this nature, you are to encamp near the enemy, and when he wishes to retire and pass the defiles in your presence, make an attack upon his rear. Much advantage is often gained by engagements of this kind.

It is also a custom to tease and tire the enemy, in order to prevent different bodies from forming a junction. The object in view sufficiently warrants such attempt, but a skilful enemy will have the address to get out of your way by a forced march, or escape the accident by taking up an advantageous position.

Sometimes when we have no inclination to fight, we are induced to it by the misconduct of the enemy, who should always be punished for his faults, if we can profit by so doing.

It must be urged, in addition to all these maxims, that our wars should ever be of short duration, and conducted with spirit, for it must always be against our interest to be engaged in a tedious affair. A long war must tend insensibly to relax our admirable discipline, depopulate our country, and exhaust its resources. For this reason, generals commanding Prussian Armies should endeavour, notwithstanding their success, to terminate every business *prudently* and *quickly*. They must not argue, as the Marshal de Luxembourg did in the Flanders wars, who, when he was told by his son, "Father, it appears to me, that we could still take another town," relied, "Hold your tongue, you little fool! would you have us go home to plant cabbages?"

In a word, on the subject of battles, we ought to be guided by the maxim of Sannerib of the Hebrews, "*that it is better one man perish than a whole people.*"

With regard to punishing an enemy for his fault, we should consult the relation of the Battle of Senef, where the Prince of Condé brought on an affair of the rear guard against the Prince of Orange or the Prince of Waldeck, who had neglected to occupy the head of a defile, in order to facilitate his retreat.

The accounts of the battle of ———, gained by the Marshal de Luxembourg, and that of Raucoux, will also furnish you with other examples.

Article 24

Of the Hazards and unforeseen Accidents which happen in War

This article would be of a melancholy length, if it was my intention to treat of all the accidents which might happen to a general in war. I shall cut the matter short by saying, that it is necessary a man should have both address and good fortune.

Generals are much more to be pitied than is generally imagined. All the world condemns them unheard. They are exposed in the gazette to the judgment of the meanest plebeian, whilst amongst many thousand readers there is not one perhaps who knows how to conduct the smallest detachment.

I shall not pretend to excuse those generals who have been in fault; I shall even give up my own campaign of 1744, but I must add, that though I have many times erred, I have made some good expeditions; for example, the siege of Prague, the defence and the retreat of Kölin, and again the retreat in Silesia. I shall not enter farther into these actions, but must observe, that there are accidents which neither the most mature reflection or keenest human foresight can possibly prevent.

As I write at present *solely* for my own generals, I shall not quote other examples than what have occurred to myself. When we were at Reichenbach, I intended to have reached the River Neiss by a forced march, and to have posted myself between the town of that name and the army of General de Neuperg, in order to cut off his communication. All the necessary dispositions were arranged for such operation, but a heavy fall of rain came on which made the roads so very bad, that our advanced guard with the pontoons were unable to proceed.

During the march of the army also, so thick a fog arose, that the troops who were posted as guards in the villages wandered about without being able to join their respective regiments. In short, everything turned out so ill, that instead of arriving at four o'clock a. m. as I had intended, we did not get there till midnight. The advantages to be derived from a forced march, were then out of the question, the enemy had the start of us, and defeated our project.

If, during your operations, diseases should break out amongst your troops, you will be obliged to act on the defensive, which was the case with us in Bohemia in the year 1741, on account of the badness of the provisions with which the troops were furnished.

At the Battle of Hohen-Friedberg, I ordered one of my *aides de-camp* (*flugel*-adjutants) to go to Margrave Charles, and tell him to place himself, as eldest general, at the head of my second line, because General Kalckstein had been detached to the command of the right wing against the Saxons: this *aide de camp* mistook the business entirely, and ordered the margrave to form the first line into the second. By great good fortune I discovered the mistake, and had time to remedy it.

Hence we see the necessity of being always on our guard, and of bearing in mind, that a commission badly, executed may disconcert all our intentions.

If a general fall sick, or be killed, at the head of a detachment of any importance, many of your measures must consequently suffer a very material derangement. To act offensively, requires generals of sound understanding and genuine valour, the number of which is but very small: I have at the most but three or four such in my whole army, if, in spite of every precaution, the enemy should succeed in depriving you of some convoy, your plans will again be disconcerted, and your project either suspended or entirely overset.

Should circumstances oblige the army to fall back, the troops will be very much discouraged.

I have never been so unhappy as to experience a situation of this sort with my *whole* army, but I remarked at the Battle of Mollwitz, that it required a length of time to reanimate troops who had been disheartened. At that time my cavalry was so weakened, that they looked on themselves as merely led to the slaughter, which induced me to send out small detachments to give them spirits, and bring them forward to action. It is only since the Battle of Hohen-Friedberg, that my cavalry are become what they ever ought to be, and what they are at present.

If the enemy should discover a spy of any consequence in their camp, the *compass* is lost which was to have directed you, and you are unable to learn anything of the enemy's movements but from your own eyes.

The negligence of officers who are detached to reconnoitre may, render your situation very distressed and embarrassing. It was in this way that Marshal de Neuperg was surprised; the *hussar* officer who was sent forward on the lookout, had neglected his duty, and we were close upon him before he had the least suspicion of it. It was also owing to the carelessness of an officer of the regiment of Ziethen in making his patrol by night, that the enemy built his bridges at Selmitz, and surprised the baggage.

Hence will appear the truth of my assertion that the safety of a whole army should never be entrusted to the vigilance of an individual officer. No one man or subaltern officer should be charged with a commission of such material consequence. Treasure up, therefore, carefully in your mind what I have said on this subject under the article, "Of the Defence of Rivers."

Too much confidence must not be reposed in patrols and reconnoitring parties, but in measures of more surety and solidity.

The greatest possible misfortune that can attend an army is *treason.* Prince Eugene was betrayed in the year 1733 by General St. ———— who had been corrupted by the French, I lost Cosel through the treachery of an officer of the garrison who deserted and conducted the enemy thither. Hence we are taught, that even in the height of our prosperity, it is not safe to trust to good fortune, or wise to be too much elevated with success; we should rather recollect, that the slender portion of genius and foresight which, we may possess is at best but a game of hazard and unforeseen accidents, by which it pleases, I know not what destiny, to humble the pride of presumptuous man.

ARTICLE 25

If it be absolutely necessary, that the General of an Army should hold a Council of War.

It was a saying of Prince Eugene, *"that if a general did not wish to fight, he had nothing more, to do than hold a council of war,"* and his assertion is proved, by the general voice of councils of war being against engaging.

Secrecy, so necessary in war, can here be no longer observed, A general, to whom his sovereign has entreated his troops, should act for himself, and the confidence placed in him by his king is a sufficient warrant for such conduct.

Nevertheless, I am persuaded that a general ought not to be inattentive to the advice of even a subaltern officer, as it is the duty of a good citizen to forget *himself* when the welfare of his country is at stake, and not regard who furnishes the advice that may be productive of happy, wished-for consequences.

ARTICLE 26

Of the Manoeuvres of an Army.

It will be seen by the maxims which I have laid down in this work, on what the theory turns of those evolutions which I have introduced amongst my troops. The object of these manoeuvres is to gain time on every occasion, and decide an affair more quickly than has heretofore been the custom; and, in short, to overset the enemy by the furious shocks of our cavalry. By means of this impetuosity, the coward is hurried away, and obliged to do his duty as well as the bravest; no single trooper can be useless. The whole depends on the *spirit* of the attack.

I therefore flatter myself that every general, convinced of the necessity and advantage of discipline, will do everything in his power to preserve and to improve it, both in the time of war and of peace.

The enthusiastic speech made by Vegece respecting the Romans, will never leave my memory:

And at length the Roman discipline triumphed over the hordes of Germans, the force of the Gauls, the German cunning, the barbarian swarm, and subdued the whole universe.

So much does the prosperity of a state depend on the discipline of its army.

ARTICLE 27

Of Winer Quarters

When a campaign is ended, we think of winter quarters, which must be arranged according to the circumstances in which we find ourselves.

The first thing to be done is, the forming the chain of troops who are to cover these quarters, which may be effected in three different ways, either behind a river, taking advantage of posts that are defended;

by mountains, or under the protection of some fortified towns.

In the year 1741-2, my troops who wintered in Bohemia, took up their position behind the Elbe. The chain which covered them began at Brandeis, and extending along by Nienbourg, Kölin, Podjebrod, and Pardubitz, ended at Kônigingraetz.

I must add here, that rivers must not be too much confided in, as when frozen they can be crossed at any point. Care should be taken to post hussars in every part of the chain to watch the enemy's movements, for which purpose, they should patrol frequently in front to observe if all be quiet, or if the enemy be assembling troops.

Besides the chain of infantry, there should be placed also brigades of cavalry and infantry here and there, to be in readiness to lend assistance wherever it might he wanted.

In the winter of 1744-5, the chain of quarters was formed the whole length of those mountains which separate Silesia from Bohemia, and we guarded very particularly the frontiers of our quarters, that we might remain in quiet.

Lieutenant-General de Trusches had to take charge of the front of Lusatia as far as the county of Glatz, the town of Sagan, and the posts from Schaniedberg to Friedland, winch last place was fortified by redoubts. There were also some other small entrenched posts on the roads of Schatzlar, Liebau, and Silberberg. The general had likewise contrived a reserve to support that post which might be first insulted by the enemy. All these detachments were covered by abbatis made in the woods, and all the roads leading into Bohemia were rendered impassable. Every post was also supplied with hussars, for the purpose of reconnoitring.

General Lehwald covered the county of Glatz with a detachment of the same nature, and with the same prudent cautions. These two generals lent each other assistance in such a way, that if the Austrians had marched against General Trusches, General Lehwald would have entered Bohemia to take the enemy in the-rear, and Trusches would have returned the favour had Lehwald been attacked.

The towns of Tropau and Jagerndorf were our highest points in Upper Silesia, and the communication was by way of Zeigenhals and Patchskau to Glatz, and by Neustadt to Ness.

It must be observed here, that we are not to trust too much to the security of mountains, but remember the proverb, "*that wherever a goat can pass a soldier can.*"

With regard to the chains of quarters that are supported by fortresses, I refer you to the winter quarters of Marshal Saxe. They are the best, but it is not in our power to choose, as the chain mast be made according to the nature of the ground which we occupy.

I shall lay it down here as a maxim, that we are never to fancy ourselves perfectly secure from the enemy's annoyance in any one town or post, but that our attention must be constantly alive to the keeping of winter quarters quiet.

Another maxim to be observed in winter quarters is, to distribute the regiments by brigades, that they may be always under the eyes of the generals.

Our service also requires, that the generals should, if possible, be with their own regiments: but there may be exceptions to this rule, of which the general commanding the army will be the best judge.

Here follow the rules that are to be observed respecting the maintenance of troops in winter quarters.

If circumstances absolutely require that we take up winter quarters in our own country, the captains and subaltern officers are to receive a gratuity proportionate to the common allowance which they receive in winter quarters. The soldier is to be famished with his bread and meat at *free cost*.

But if the winter quarters are in an enemy's country, the general in chief of the troops shall receive 15,000 florins, the generals of the cavalry and infantry 10,000 each, lieutenants generals 7000, major-generals (camp marshals) 5000, captains of cavalry 2000, of infantry 1800, and the subaltern officers 100 *ducats* or from 400 to 500 florins. The country is to supply the soldier with bread, flesh, and beer *gratis*, but he is to have no moneys as that only tends to favour desertion.

The general in chief is to take care that this business be properly arranged, and that no pillaging be allowed, but he is not to be too strict with an officer who has it in his power to make any trifling, *fair* advantage.

If the army be quartered in an enemy's country, it is the duty of the general commanding to see that the necessary number of recruits be furnished: (such distribution should obtain in the circles, that three regiments, for example, should be assigned to one, and four to the other.) Each circle should also be subdivided into regiments, as is done in the enrolling cantonments.

If the recruits are furnished voluntarily by the States of the country, so much the better; if not, compulsive methods must be used. They ought to arrive very early, that the officer may have time to drill them

Preussen.

Grenadier.   Musketier.   Offizier.

Infanterie-Regiment von Forcade
(1806 v. Winning, No. 23).
1756.

and make them fit for duty the following spring. This, however, is not to prevent the captain from sending out recruiting parties.

As the general in chief ought to interest himself in the whole of this economy, he should be particularly careful that the artillery horses and the provisions, which are a tribute of the country, are furnished in kind or in hard cash.

All the baggage waggons, and, in short, the whole apparatus of an army, is also to be repaired at the enemy's cost.

Minute attention must be paid by the general that the cavalry officers repair their saddles, bridles, stirrups, and boots, and that the officers of infantry provide their men with shoes, stockings, shirts, and *gaitres* for the ensuing campaign. The soldiers' blankets and tents should also be repaired, the cavalry swords filed, and the arms of the infantry put in good condition. The artillery, likewise, must prepare the necessary quantity of cartridges for the infantry.

It still remains to be seen by the general, that the troops which form the chain are well provided with powder and ball, and, in short, that nothing be wanting in the whole army.

If time allow, the general would do well to visit some of his quarters, to examine into the state of the troops, and satisfy himself that the officers attend to the exercising of their men, as well as to every other part of their duty: for it is necessary that the old soldiers should be employed in this way as well as the recruits, in order to keep them in practice.

At the beginning of a campaign, we change the cantoning quarters, and distribute them according to the order of battle, *viz.* the cavalry on the wings, and the infantry in the centre. These cantonments generally extend nine or ten leagues (from four to five miles) in front, to four (two) in depth, and when the time of encamping draws near, they are to be contracted a little.

I find it very convenient in cantonments to distribute the troops in orders of the six eldest generals: one, for example, shall command all the cavalry of the right wing, and another that of the left, in the first line, whilst two others shall command that of the second. In this method, all orders will more quickly be executed, and the troops be more easily formed into columns to go to camp.

On the subject of winter quarters, I must again advise you to be very careful of not going into them before you are well convinced that the enemy's army is entirely departed. Keep always in your recollection the misfortune which befell the Elector Frederick William, when he was surprised by the Marshal de Turenne in his quarters at Alsace.

ARTICLE 28

Of Winter Campaigns in particular,

Winter campaigns ruin the troops, both on account of the diseases which they occasion, and by obliging them to be constantly in motion, which prevents their being well cloathed or recruited. The same inconvenience attends the carriage of ammunition and provisions.

It is certain, that the best army in the world cannot long support campaigns of this kind, for which reason they ought ever to be avoided, as being, of all expeditions, the most to be condemned. Accidents, however, may occur, which will oblige a general to undertake them.

I believe that I have made more winter campaigns than any general of this age, and that I shall do right to explain the motives which induced me to such undertakings.

At the death of the Emperor Charles VI. in the year 1740, there were but two Austrian regiments in all Silesia. Having determined to make good the claims of my house on that duchy, I was obliged to make war in winter, that I might profit by every favourable circumstance, and carry the theatre of war to the Neiss,

If I had delayed my project till the spring, the war would have been established between Crossen and Glogau, and it would have required three or four hard campaigns to effect that which we accomplished by one simple march. This reason appeared to me sufficiently cogent.

If I did not succeed in the winter campaign which I made in the year 1742 to relieve the country from the Elector of Bavaria, it was because the French behaved like fools, and the Saxons like traitors.

My third winter campaign in the year 1741-2 was forced upon me, as I was obliged to drive the Austrians from Silesia, which they had invaded.

From the beginning of the winter 1745-6, the Austrians and Saxons wished to introduce themselves into my hereditary dominions, that they might put everything to fire and sword—I acted according to my usual principle, and got the start of them by making war in the middle of winter in the very heart of their own country.

Should similar circumstances occur, I should not hesitate to pursue the same plan, and shall applaud the conduct of my generals who shall follow my example. But I must ever blame those who, without the concurrence of such reasons, shall undertake a war at that season of the year.

In regard to the detail of winter campaigns, the troops are always to be as close to each other as possible, in their cantonments, and two or three regiments of cavalry, mixed with infantry, should be lodged in one village, if it be large enough to hold them. Sometimes all the infantry are quartered in one town, as the Prince of Anhalt did at Torgau, Eilenbourg, Meissen, and two or three other small towns (whose names I forget) in Saxony, after which he encamped himself.

When we come near the enemy, a *rendezvous* is to be appointed to the troops, who are to continue marching as before in several columns; and when about to make any decisive movements, such as, storming the enemy's quarters, or marching against him to engage, we arrange ourselves in order of battle, remaining under the canopy of heaven, each company kindling a large fire, by which to pass away the night. But as such fatigues are too distressing to be long endured, all possible dispatch should be employed in enterprises of this nature. We must not stand contemplating one danger or hesitating about it, but form our resolution with *spirit* and execute it with *firmness*.

Be careful of undertaking a winter campaign in a country which is crowded with fortified places, for the season will prevent your setting down seriously before a place which you cannot carry by surprise. We may be assured beforehand that such a project will miscarry, as it is morally impossible it should be otherwise.

If it be left: to our choice, the troops should have as much rest during the winter as possible, and the time should be employed to the best advantage in recovering the army, that at the opening of the campaign they may get the start of their adversaries.

These are nearly the principal rules of the grand manoeuvres of war, the particulars of which have been explained as much as was in my power. I have taken particular care that what I have said should be clear and intelligible, but if any parts should, in your idea, still remain obscure, I shall be favoured by your communicating them, that I may either explain myself more, fully, or subscribe to your opinion, if it prove better than mine own.

The small experience of war which has fallen to my share, convinces me, that it is an art never to be exhausted), but that something new will ever reward his labour who studies it with serious application.

I shall not think my moments misemployed if what I have said should stimulate my officers to the study of that science, which will afford them the most certain opportunity of acquiring glory, rescuing their names from the rust of oblivion, and securing by their brilliant actions a glorious and immortal fame.

Particular Instruction of the King of Prussia to the Officers of His Army, and especially those of the Cavalry

Preussen.

v. Natzmer-Ulanen.

1740—1742.

Preface
To Officers

Many people wish to command, and fancy themselves equal to the undertaking, without knowing if they possess a necessary share of experience and of the other requisites, and without having learned to be commanded themselves.

This circumstance obtains particularly in the military life, and especially amongst young officers. But if they knew that very often the fault of a moment, or even the slightest mistake, may destroy a reputation gained by years of trouble and fatigue, and especially that during a campaign, such faults are irremediable, and punishment their natural consequence, they would certainly be more anxious to obtain such knowledge, than to be placed in situations that demand its practice, without their having acquired it. Experience and good conduct will certainly lead to honour, which every other path tends to error and mistake.

The obedience and subordination to which youth for a certain time are subject, subdue the passions peculiar to that age: hence danger becomes familiar to the soldier, and he is rendered intrepid and capable of forming at a moment any resolution which circumstances may require: by this means also he becomes inured to the fatigues of war, and takes delight in his profession, convinced that his advancement therein depends upon it. Through this, the officer also learns to be acquainted with the individuals whom he is one day to command, and by gaining their esteem and confidence, ensures the prompt and zealous execution of his orders.

Every officer should bear in mind, that the true point of honour alone may prove the foundation of his fortune: he should therefore constantly regard it as the *main-spring* of all his actions, and be fully persuaded, that it is the only road by which he can arrive at those honourable distinctions which are the just reward of real desert. The true point of honour will ever induce him, not only to avoid all imputation of *blame*, but also to endeavour to procure esteem by his own personal merit: it is this which will convince him that it is not only necessary to signalise himself when an occasion offers, but that it in the duty of every intelligent officer to search and be on the look-out for such opportunity.

It should also be his particular study to observe and make himself well acquainted with all the proceedings and schemes which may have been conceived by the enemy, or are likely so to foe, that he may be able to frustrate or destroy them, seize a favourable moment fair attack, weaken or disturb them as circumstances may allow. Of this one maxim he ought never to lose sight, that much zeal is necessary in the execution of every enterprise, and that there is always some attendant risk.

Grounded in these principles he will avoid placing too much confidence in his own strength or knowledge, and consider that he can undertake or perform nothing without the assistance of his comrades, whose duty it is to support him on all occasions, it therefore becomes very essential, that he endeavour to know them, and be capable of judging the extent of each individual's capacity in his profession. He should also court the confidence and friendship of valuable men, especially amongst those who are under his own command, and be able to distinguish the particular kind of service for which each man seems adapted: for example, some hussars are very clever at reconnoitring an enemy, who know nothing of reconnoitring a country; and again, others may perform this last service very well, though unable, from some bodily infirmity, to execute the former; as in this case it often happens that many such feeding nights are of necessity passed under the canopy of heaven or in a wood, there are also, who conduct themselves much better on patrols or skirmishing parties than in a regular action.

All that has been said respecting the private soldier, applies with equal force and justice to the officer. If in any affair he knows how to conduct himself agreeably to the dispositions of the people under him, the execution of it will be more easy, pleasant, and certain. There are in every squadron some old cunning troopers, who can often furnish excellent ideas, and make very valuably discoveries, if an opportunity be allowed them; with such, therefore, an officer would do well to converse, as he will not only derive instruction from their communications, but also secure the friendship and confidence of the private soldier, which, in all expeditions, may prove of the highest advantage.

Moreover, he should endeavour to distinguish the courageous soldier from him who is less so, that he may know, on an emergency, whom to select. The good soldier should be particularly noticed, and his every want supplied: by this means he becomes attached to his officer, who will be sure to reap glory and honour from his services. The weak and inexperienced men should also be encouraged, who will sometimes, in consequence, attempt such actions as appear at first sight to be dictated by rashness.

No officer should propose to himself a certain degree of rank which is to terminate his career, for he will then spare no pains, and neglect no means to gain his point; and if he cannot pretend to it on the score of abilities, he will have recourse to powerful interest, which supplies his defect of merit, and procures for him the situation which he wishes. Hence we often see officers, who, for a certain time, are at infinite and almost incredible pains, as soon as they attain the object of their pursuit, fall off, and go through their duty with the greatest imaginable indifference. No justness or choice influences the actions and orders of such officers, and as they depend entirely on chance, their reputation, of consequence, frequently falls a sacrifice. Nothing is more certain, than that the man who enters the service from any other motive than that of honour, if he seek riches or his own personal interest, will become a prey do avarice or some other despicable passion, which will render him an object of hatred and contempt.

Nothing injures an officer more in the opinion of a soldier than the suspicion of fraud: this is often induced by a passion for *play*, the fatal consequences of which too often extend much farther: his money had much better be expended in the purchase of good arms or good horses, on which the life and reputation of a man so often depend.

An officer should possess an equal share of sobriety and reserve: with these two qualities, he will not only save his purse from unnecessary drains, but be always ready and disposed to do his duty whenever called upon. He should regard himself as a model for those beneath him, who are generally sufficiently ready in copying their superiors. Should an officer, in particular, be addicted to drinking, or any vice of that nature, the soldier, who readily perceives it, will certainly not endeavour to correct it in himself, and will think it very hard to be rebuked for it, nor can the officer expostulate with him on the business without signing his own condemnation. The true foundation and ground-work of a good officer is a virtuous irreproachable conduct, not merely superficial, by serving as a guide to all his actions, for nothing can be more contradictory to real valour, than an embarrassed conscience.

Now that I have laid down the means of making a good officer, I proceed to shew how he is to conduct himself in a campaign, (particularly if he be in the cavalry), and point out the sure and certain path to honour and to glory.

The Second Treatise

ARTICLE 1
Of advanced Guards.

When the whole of an army, or a part of it, is on the march, the guards in front and rear, as well as the flank patrols, are furnished by the light troops. They are intended also, for the most part, to form the advanced guards. When the army is arrived at the ground of encampment, the guard in front divides itself into several parties, so extended as to cover the whole front of the camp, whilst the infantry are employed in pitching tents and posting sentries. The same precautions are to be observed by the rear guard and flank patrols.

Whilst the army is thus employed, it is the peculiar business of the light troops that are advanced to send forward patrols to search and scour minutely all the woods, copses, ravines, or defiles that may be in their front, and it may be, occupied by the enemy, who, taking advantage of the army's being employed in arranging their camp, might fall upon it, and throw it into confusion. When all this business is finished, and the camp properly settled, the major-general of the day, or some other commanding officer, arrives, places the guards, and appoints to every officer his proper post.

All the advanced posts should be so contrived, that the piquets be placed on elevated situations and concealed by trees: the main body of the guard should be posted seven, eight, or nine hundred paces in the rear of the piquets, either in some small wood or behind houses, to prevent being seen, and their force discovered by the enemy, but the advanced guards should never allow the piquets to be out of their sight.

When the officer has taken possession of his post, and the advanced guards are properly placed, if he be a stranger to the country, he must procure a man from some neighbouring house or village, and question him (whilst he carefully examines his map of the country) concerning the names of the surrounding villages, if there be in the neighbourhood any defiles, swamps, ravines, or other necessary objects of his attention: he must also carefully observe all the roads and bye-paths that are in his front, enquiring particularly whither they lead, if passable by cannon, and if the enemy can advance to his post by any indirect approach. He must get himself informed of all these particulars as minutely as possible, that he may be qualified to give satisfactory answers if called upon, be able to take proper measures if occasion present, and give particular instructions to his patrols who are to march in front.

When he is perfectly acquainted with these circumstances, he must repair to his vedettes, who should always be double on each post, and assign to each his peculiar charge, on what part of the neighbourhood he is continually to have his eye, especially on the ravines, causeways, or villages.

These dispositions having taken place, and the posts sufficiently instructed, if there be time, the officer may allow the advanced guard to dismount, and feed their horses. But if his post be not perfectly secure, one half of the detachment must remain saddled and bridled till the other half are fed and mounted. No feeding or dismounting is to be allowed at night, as *that* is supposed to have taken place just before dark; so that during the night the horses may be saddled and bridled, and at least one half mounted, to be prepared for any accident that may happen.

If the main body of the advanced guard should be placed near a village, the commanding officer may send a man or two to the top of the steeple, or of some high house, that he may be able to discover the enemy, and by discharging a pistol, give notice of their approach.

When the general of the camp comes near the advanced guard, they are to mount and advance their carbines; but if the body of the guard be so situate as to be entirely discernible by the enemy, it will not be advisable to mount, as the enemy will thereby be informed of the presence of the general or some superior officer, who may, in consequence, be disturbed in the visiting of his posts. If any detachment passes in front of an advanced guard, the guard also mount and advance their carbines.

The officer must scrupulously examine all persons who come towards his post from without, of whoever degree, whether peasants or travellers; enquiring whence they come, whither they we going, what their business in camp or elsewhere, or if they have any knowledge of the enemy or their situation; after which he will either suffer them to pass on, or send them back, agreeably to the orders he has received. He must conduct himself in the same manner towards the people who bring provisions into the camp, and, if he be forbidden to suffer them to pass, send them back in a civil manner, doing everything in his power to conciliate the affections of the inhabitants, as by this means he may often gain information very material to the army.

The officer must visit his vedettes both by night and day, enquiring of them what their duty is on that post, and what they have observed there, to convince himself that they are properly acquainted with their charge. He should also be provided with a good spy-glass, to enable him to reconnoitre the environs of his post. During the night, his posts are to be visited *hourly* by a non-commissioned officer, and *once* by himself, to keep his people waking and alert.

If an advanced guard be placed so near the enemy as to be able to discover all their movements, much attention is required to discern if any number of troops arrive, what they are, if they again quit the camp, and what route they take. Troops are often detached from the enemy's camp, especially from the second or third line, without striking tents, the better to conceal their march.

It is for this reason, that an officer commanding an advanced guard is required to be particularly attentive, to be provided with a very good glass, and when such event takes place, to report it immediately to the general commanding. This precaution is more particularly necessary at daybreak, that he may be assured whether the enemy's camp retain its old position, or if any change has taken place in the night.

By night it is easy to discover if troops enter or leave the camp, by the noise that is made: their arrival will be known by the clashing of fire-arms, the voices of the waggoners and artillery drivers, the cracking of whips, and the neighing of horses. If there be any cavalry amongst them, it will also be manifested by the driving in of picquet-posts, and the lighting of fires. In this case the officer should be constantly in front, perfectly quiet, and observing all that passes. But if the army or a part of it *decamp* during the night, it will be discovered, in addition to the foregoing circumstances, by the gradual decrease of noise, and lessening brightness of the fires. To this last circumstance, however, it is not always prudent to trust, as the fires are often kept up by the light troops after the army has decamped.

When the army moves by day, the advanced guards should mount at the moment that the drums beat to march, watching the enemy, and moving forward as soon as their posts are fallen back, and have formed (as they generally do) the rear guard. The moment of departure for the advanced guards is at all times to be ordered by the general commanding. On these occasions no particular movement is to be made before the time, but they are to remain in their former position till the moment of departure, for by repeated movements, or too much hurry in mounting, the enemy may conceive that the army is retreating, and send immediately some troops in its pursuit. It is not even necessary that the private soldier should be informed of what is going forward; for which reason an officer or non-commissioned officer must be sent round in proper time to relieve at once all the detached posts and vedettes.

As soon as the vedettes perceive the approach of an enemy's party, they are to fire: he that has fired is then to hasten instantly to the advanced guards and report what he has seen: the guard ready and concealed, will remain on its post, sending forward a non-commissioned officer with a few men to reconnoitre the force of the enemy, and then reporting immediately to the general commanding all that has passed, that he may make his dispositions accordingly, and reinforce the advanced guard if necessary.

It often happens that the generals of the enemy approach the advanced guard under an escort, in order to dislodge the vedettes from their heights, that they may gain possession of them, and reconnoitre our camp. As soon as the officer commanding shall be informed of this by his vedettes, he must betake himself to the spot, and if he see several people approaching the height under an escort, send the intelligence instantly to the general officer under whose orders he acts, exerting himself to the utmost of his power in defence of the height, that the enemy may not become possessed of it and discover the situation of our camp.

When a trumpeter from the enemy's camp, either alone or accompanied by an officer, comes towards a vedette and sounds a parley, one of the vedettes must advance towards him and conduct him to his post, placing him with his face towards the country from whence he came, to prevent his discovering anything in our camp to our disadvantage: a vedette is then to repair to the officer commanding the advanced guard, and to report him, who will immediately go himself or send a non-commissioned officer to blind his eyes and conduct him to his post. He is then to enquire of him the object of his visit, report it to the general, and obtain his leave to conduct him to the camp. The same ceremonies are to be observed with respect to deserters from the enemy, who are to have their arms taken from them at the advanced guard, and be conducted to the general commanding under a proper escort. This circumstance happening at night furnishes an additional reason for attending particularly to these cautions.

When an advanced guard is placed with a deep ditch, river, or brook in its front, the officer commanding the post is to survey the whole length of his district, to discover if there be any bridges or fords which render the passage easy; if so, he will place his vedettes in such a manner as to prevent the enemy from taking advantage of such circumstance to fall upon him. In this case, the vedettes are not to be drawn in at night, as they generally are, but to remain constantly on their posts. The bridge should be stripped, and the planks laid by, in readiness to be replaced if any detachments or patrols should have occasion to pass. During the night, small patrols should be pushed the whole extent of the ditches or rivulets, marching with great caution and circumspection, and if the bank be much covered with brambles, stopping frequently and listening to find if there be any rustling amongst them, as a company of infantry might easily lie there concealed, and annoy the patrols.

It is to be observed as a general rule, that the vedettes are on no account whatever to be placed out of sight of each other.

Towards the close of the evening, the officer commanding the advanced guard must report by a non-commissioned officer all that he has observed at his post, and also all that he has learnt from the peasants or his patrols: to be correct in this, he would do right to commit to paper the occurrences of the day, and, if necessary, make his report in writing. At the same time, he will learn the *parole* and *countersign*. The *countersign* is to be given to each vedette the moment he is posted, which win take place every hour, or every two hours, according to the season and the weather. Neither the *parole*, or any order of material import, is to be. imparted by the officer to any person whatever.

When the darkness of the night prevents a distant view, and especially in the vicinity of the enemy's posts, the officer must fall back with his detachment two or three hundred paces; the vedettes also must do the same, still preserving a convenient distance

When the night is perfectly obscure, the horses are not to be allowed to feed, or even to be unbridled. If occasion require, or if from contiguity of situation, a surprise be to be feared, the detachment should remain mounted the whole night. If there be no danger, a part way dismount, and if the season require, and circumstances allow, a little fire may be kindled, provided it be in a hollow place, and not easily to be discovered. On the least alarm, the fire is to be extinguished, to effect which, earth or sand may be used for want of water, otherwise it would serve as a guide to the enemy, and prove an annoyance to the post.

The officer commanding an advanced guard should be particularly attentive to the keeping his people waking and alert, not allowing them in any account whatever to sleep, or fasten their horse, but hold them by the end of the halter, with the reigns of the bit and bridon on the saddle, that, at the first signal, they may be in readiness to mount.

Small patrols, according to the strength of the guard, are to be sent in front of the vedettes every hour, or oftener, if necessary, who will advance two hundred paces beyond the vedettes and traverse their whole front, halting frequently to discover if there be any noise or footstep near; if it be the case, one of the patrol is to return immediately with the report to the advanced guard, whilst the remainder place themselves as near the noise as possible, to discover the cause: if it prove to proceed from a party of the enemy, the patrol will fire and fall back quickly, under cover of the night, on the grand guard.

Whenever the vedettes hear any noise by night, one of them should advance four or five hundred paces, challenge and demand the *countersign*, and if he receives no answer, he should fire and fall back quickly.

When troops detached from camp approach the vedettes, they are not to be allowed to come within the line, even though they be provided with the *countersign*: the commanding officer of the advanced guard must order the officer of the detachment to come forward in charge of a non-commissioned officer and two men, and question him minutely, (unless be happen to know him personally,) making him remain with him whilst his detachment files off towards the camp; as soon as the detachment has passed the post, the officer may be permitted ;to follow. But if it happen that the detachment has been many days absent from camp, and consequently ignorant of the *countersign*, it behoves the officer commanding the advanced guard to redouble his care and diligence in making the most scrupulous examination, and if he find no reason to the contrary, he may suffer the detachment to file off one by one, in front of his guard.

If an advanced guard should not be able, for want of sufficient strength, to extend properly its vedettes, particularly if the country be hilly or intersected with many little valleys or defiles, or the night should be dark and gloomy, the vedettes must visit each other alternately from right to left, taking care that one be always fixed on his post, that nothing may pass unobserved in the hollow ways: on these occasions, the patrols should also be on the march, and the advanced guard constantly in motion.

It frequently happens, that a general wishing to reconnoitre the enemy, takes the officer of the advanced guard with him in front of his post, as a protection: in this case, the officer, leaving his vedettes on their posts, must form with the remainder of his party a guard in front of the general, and patrols on his flanks, to cover him and his suite: if the general proceed the whole length of the line, the officer must keep himself four or five hundred paces towards the enemy on the general's flank, in such a manner that he may be always covered: besides this, he may detach a part of his troop towards the enemy, who, marching by the general one by one, at certain distances, with their eyes constantly looking towards the enemy, will prevent anything from approaching to the annoyance of the general whilst making his discoveries. When the general is returned to camp, and safe within the line, the officer may return to his post.

When an officer commanding an advanced guard has reason to expect an attack by night, he must give such instructions to his vedettes and non-commissioned officers that are detached, that if the accident should arrive, they may not fall back immediately on his post, but a little to one side of it. The advantage arising from this caution will be, that the enemy, though superior in numbers, will not have it in their power to fall on the main body with the whole front of their party, or even attack them on the flank or in the rear, and put them to route by favour of the night. In these circumstances, the advanced guard are to keep tip a constant firing, and to retire very slowly, skirmishing as they go, to allow time for the troops who are ordered to their support to arrive, and that the army may have proper notice of the enemy's approach.

If any man of the advanced guard should desert during the night, the officer must immediately change the *countersign*, and send it to the piquets and vedettes, lest the enemy, profiting by such intelligence, might present themselves as friends, and surprise the detachment. The same rule should also be observed on any desertion whatever. It is likewise very material, that he change the position of his troop, lest the deserter may conduct the enemy immediately upon him.

It often happens during the night, that the army decamps very quietly, either on an expedition or from some other motive, leaving their advanced guards on their post till daybreak, to conceal their intentions from the enemy: in this case the greatest circumspection is required, that no patrol of the enemy approach and discover it's being marched. To effect this, the whole of the guard should be mounted, and small patrols be constantly moving four or five hundred paces in front of the vedettes, to hinder their approach. But if at daybreak, the enemy should discover what has happened, the officer must draw in his posts insensibly, and betake himself to the station assigned him, leaving a non-commissioned officer as a rear guard to cover him in the same manner that he covers the army.

His eyes should nevertheless be often turned behind him, to discover if the enemy follow, in what force, and what troops they are, which circumstances he is to report to the officer commanding the rear guard. It happens too often, that on quitting their ground, the soldiers, servants, women, or other followers of the camp, set fire, to the huts, discovering by such practice the march of the army. The greatest attention and most positive orders must be enjoined to prevent such accidents.

If an advanced guard be placed in a very hilly country, it is not enough that it is covered in front of the enemy, but the officer must also visit during the day all the neighbourhood, to select proper situations in the low places and copses for night-posts, where he may be safe from being surprised or surrounded: the patrols also should visit during the night every situation where there is any kind of danger.

When an officer, placed in a country with which he is unacquainted, receives orders during the night to change the position of his guard, he is not to do it instantly without care or caution, but first have recourse to his map by a light procured from an adjacent house, or some other means, and examine particularly the neighbourhood to which he is about to remove. The situation of his main guard, his vedettes, and the route his patrols are to take, should be particularly clear and manifest to him. He should endeavour to lay hold of some countryman, learn from him all necessary circumstances, be conducted by him to the ground which he has observed on his map, and then post his vedettes according to the plan that he has formed.

Finding himself in a strange country, and particularly if there be an enemy in the neighbourhood, he must keep his party mounted all night, constantly sending out patrols.

At daybreak, when he is able to look about him, the little errors and mistakes which took place owing, to the darkness of the night, may be rectified. The safety and security of an entire army often depends on the vigilance and intelligence of an officer commanding an outpost or detachment. He ought consequently to pay the most particular attention to the exact execution of his duty, as the least negligence on his part may be productive of the most disastrous consequences, both to himself and the whole army. Supposing, indeed, that he should be attacked by a force greatly superior to his own, it is his duty to maintain his post as long as possible, and if forced at length to retire, it should be done coolly, skirmishing and keeping up a constant fire, that the body of the army which he covers may have time to take up a good position, and be well prepared to receive the enemy.

It is a general custom for the new guard to advance at day-break within five or six hundred paces of the old guard, to support it in case of an attack, which often happens at that period. If all be quiet, the new guard advances, and *salutes* at the distance of five hundred pates, taking ground to the left. The officer commanding the old guard gives the word to *mount,* and to *salute,* as soon as he sees the new guard arrive. The two officers then meet each other, and the relieving officer learns from the retiring one all the necessary particulars. The officer of the new guard choses and appoints the men that are necessary as vedettes, and, followed by a non-commissioned officer, learns from the officer of the old guard the situation of the posts.

A non-commissioned officer should attend him, that he may be informed how to place and to relieve the posts. This business being settled, every particular communicated, and all the patrols of the old guard called in, it files off, and at the distance of one hundred paces, *recovers arms*; the new guard immediately comes also to the recover. The one officer conducts his party in good order to the regiment, and presents himself to the general commanding, whilst the other takes possession of the spot occupied by the old guard, and orders his people to dismount.

ARTICLE 2

Of Patrols and Reconnoitrings

Patrols are of two kinds, those that, are made by night, and those by day. The difference between the two consists only in the manner of making them. I shall now proceed to give a concise idea of what ought to be the conduct of a commissioned or non-commissioned officer, who is ordered to take charge of a patrol by day.

When a commissioned or non-commissioned officer shall be ordered with five or six men to endeavour to make observations on the enemy's camp, or to reconnoitre a part of the country near the enemy, he must detach one of his most trusty men four or five hundred paces in front; if it be in a flat country, he may send another man to the same distance on that side where he supposes the enemy to be placed, and if danger be to be apprehended on both sides, a third may be detached to the other side at the same distance. These men must march in a parallel line with the main body; but if the day should prove foggy, the advanced guard and flank patrols would do well rather to approach the main body, than keep at a distance from it, to prevent their being cut off, or inclining too much to one side.

In dark cloudy weather, firing is of very little service; in these circumstances, therefore, a more than common share of caution is necessary.

Nevertheless, it sometimes happens, that patrols can be pushed with the greatest advantage under cover of a fog.

If there should be discovered on the sides of the heights any copses or villages at more than four or five hundred paces distance, the patrols are not to go absolutely into them, but to approach them very nearly, and if nothing be to be discovered by this means, they will pass quietly along the skirts of the woods or villages, to learn if they are occupied by any party of the enemy.

If a detachment, whether large or small, be obliged to enter a forest, the men marching on the flanks must keep so near as not to lose sight of the main body of the party. The man who is in front of all, must always maintain the same distance, searching all the bushes and thickets that he meets with, and paying the greatest possible attention to whatever he sees or hears. If a hill or any height should be before him, he must creep up very quietly, and look very narrowly all around, him; and, if no party of the enemy or any other object of impediment be to be discovered, continue his route.

If a commissioned or non-commissioned officer be detached with eight, ten, or twelve men, he must always send two men four or five hundred paces in front; and on whatever side he expects the enemy, he will for safety have a man on each flank, who must attend to the foregoing instructions.

If we pass by: a forest, two men should be stationed at such a distance in the rear, as never to lose sight of the main body of the party, to prevent thereby a surprise from the enemy in that quarter, if any should be concealed in the wood.

The two men who are sent forward, may march side by side in a flat country, but if a village or small wood should be in their fronts one must proceed some hundred panes before the other to survey such object; the second man should follow at a regular distance, traversing the whole extent of these objects, observing the same cautions with the man before him, that he may discover the enemy, though they may have been passed unperceived by the other.

If these two men should arrive at a mountain or height, they are not both to ascend it, but one is to advance at a gallop, observing all the afore-mentioned rules for the discovery of the enemy: if he sees nothing, he is to remain on the summit till the other man, at a walk, has joined him, where they may pursue their route as before. If the man in front or on the flanks perceive the enemy without being dis-covered themselves, they are to fall back immediately on the body of the party without firing, that they may take some other route without being observed.

But if these men meet the enemy, and are perceived by them, they are immediately to give notice of it, by discharge of musket or pistol; and, if they be not too suddenly surprised, and their retreat to the party cut off, hasten to report to the commissioned or non-commis-sioned officer what they have seen: and as detachments of this kind are not always intended for fighting or engagement with the. enemy, the officer commanding must fall back with his party as soon as he is assured by discharge of pistol of the presence of the enemy, without waiting to be informed by any of his people who are upon the flanks.

If the man who has met the enemy escapes being taken, he should join his detachment as soon as possible, and report what he has seen.

If the officer find that the enemy advances upon him, and is supe-rior in number, he is not to wait their arrival to risk an engagement, but disperse his people one by one, before the enemy be too near.

These scattered men must endeavour to gain the woods or villages; for it is hardly to be supposed that the enemy will follow them thither, from a fear that a *corps de reserve* lies there concealed. This is often the case, and naturally proves fatal to the enemy that are too eager in their pursuit. Indeed, though a few men should be taken in a retreat of this kind; some will remain to report to the general or the officer who sent out the detachment; whereas, if they retreated in a body, it is more than probable that everyone would be taken.

When a commissioned or non-commissioned officer is ordered to march with two, three, or four men into a country occupied by a party of the enemy, he must avoid the high roads, and even the bye-paths that are much trodden, and steal along, if the country will allow it, by the sides of bushes and in hollow places, where he and his people may be covered. In this case, he must not regard how much he winds about, so that he ultimately attains the object of his mission. If in his march he meet with any heights, he must halt his people, and ascend them alone very gently, looking on every side for the enemy: if all be safe, he should silently pursue his route, attending to the foregoing instructions. If this expedition be undertaken by night, it is to be conducted in the manner which will hereafter be explained.

Every person who is met by the advanced guard, or the flank patrols, should be conducted to the officer commanding the detachment, to be by him examined; and if they were going towards the enemy, they should be kept under charge of two or three men in the rear, as long as the officer may think necessary to prevent their giving to the enemy any intelligence of his operations.

An officer sent on a reconnoitring party (where it is his duty to get as near the enemy as he conveniently can) should decline, on his march through suspected places, any kind of engagement with the enemy, unless it be absolutely unavoidable. On the discovery of an enemy's patrol, he should do all in his power to avoid them, even though he be superior in force, and much less should he busy himself in plundering or taking prisoners, as by those means he would certainly be discovered, the enemy fall upon him, and his project miscarry.

If it be an object to gain a height which is in possession of the enemy, it should be approached as quietly and as closely as possible, and then attacked with the greatest precipitation to dislodge the enemy; and, after all the necessary observations have been made, the party should retire through bye-paths and covered ways. In an expedition of this kind, it would be prudent to leave in the rear at a certain distance from the enemy, along the side of a village, or hedge through which the party must again pass, a few men with some of the worst horses, and, if possible, those that are white, that they may be seen at a distance, and give the idea to the enemy who are pursuing the patrol, of a corps de reserve being posted there. This will abate their ardour of pursuit, and give the patrol time to save itself.

A trumpeter also may be placed behind a hill, who should shew himself and sound a march when he sees the patrol closely pressed, to make the enemy believe that a *corps de reserve* is concealed also on that side. The men who are left behind, on seeing their comrades pursued, should shew themselves now on one side of the bushes, and now on the other, with the appearance of reconnoitring. They may also now and then discharge a pistol, as if to give notice to troops behind them, of the enemy's approach. When the patrols come near them, they are to be the first to retreat with the *bad* horses. If this scheme should not succeed, but that the enemy still continues the pursuit, the officer should order his people to disperse making them well acquainted with the place of *rendezvous*.

In patrols of this nature, the retreat ought never to be conducted with too much hurry, but now and then a halt to be made, and a face shewn to the enemy at every, defile or, bridge, to endeavour to keep them in check, suffer the *bad* horses.to gain ground, and the *good* ones to get wind. The pursuing enemy should always be kept upon a run to put their horses out of wind, but if they also are found to come near the defile or bridge, the party should retire very alertly, so as not to give them an opportunity of slackening their pace. If, in these circumstances, there be any bridges or villages to pass, the former, if the enemy be not too near, should be stripped or destroyed, and the entrance to the latter *barricadoed* with poles, pieces of timber, carriages, or whatever is near at hand; the *good* horses will always be able to follow fast enough, and the enemy will find themselves checked.

In a word, an officer should do his utmost to prevent any of his people being taken unguardedly, or through his negligence, for the losses to which light troops are *daily* subject, fall sufficiently heavy, and though *men* are readily replaced, it is no easy matter to procure *seasoned soldiers*. An officer should also be particularly careful that his people do not tarry in the villages at the doors of the public houses, and that all his orders are executed with the greatest exactness.

When an officer is sent in front on an expedition of this kind, he ought to avoid going through the villages as much as possible, even though they may have been scoured by his advanced guard. If he must of necessity pass them, it must be done cautiously, halting at a convenient distance till the advanced guard has made its report. This report alone, however, is not to satisfy him, but he must visit in person every barn and stable, to convince himself that no enemy lies there concealed: for it often happens, that an enemy will suffer a patrol to pass, cut off its retreat, and fall with advantage on the main body of the party.

Two men should be left as a guard on each defile or bridge, which is to be passed and repassed towards the enemy, who by a frequent discharge of pistol are to inform the officer commanding the detachment, if the enemy, who lay concealed as he went forward, should wish to take possession of the bridges or defiles, and cut off his retreat: in such case, these men are to retire immediately. If an accident of this kind should happen to an officer, he ought to be prepared beforehand, from his knowledge of other bridges or fords, learnt from his map or otherwise, to make good his retreat without falling into the hands of the enemy.

The same line of conduct should also be observed with respect to rivers, whose banks are to be traversed when patrolling on the side of the enemy.

Possession should be kept of all the bridge, and every avenue guarded, so that if the enemy should approach with a view to cut off the retreat, the detachment, informed of it by discharge of pistol, may take another route. No harm can arise from weakening the detachment by this means, as on these occasions they are not designed to fight.

Provided that care be taken of the men and horses, and that the soldier is convinced that you feel an interest in his comfort and safety on every occasion, you are sure to gain the confidence and goodwill of all who are under your command.

The people who are left behind to guard the bridges and the avenues, have nothing to fear except from their own negligence, as, on the approach of the enemy, they have always sufficient time to retire.

Every officer who is ordered on an expedition of this nature, should exert himself to execute his commission with all possible prudence, and reconnoitre minutely whatever he sees. If he be to reconnoitre the enemy's camp, to discover it's situation, to learn how it is protected on each side, whether by a river, wood, mountain, swamp, or village, he ought to know of how many lines it is composed, the extent of its front, the situation of headquarters, and the park of artillery; whether the camp be entrenched, what are the names of the villages in front, rear, and on the flanks; if the enemy has any advanced posts, of what troops composed, and where placed; if the neighbouring towns and villages furnish the camp with provisions and forage, what articles they deliver, and in what quantity. These are questions which will certainly be put to him by the general commanding, whose dispositions will be influenced by his answers.

Nothing can reflect so much discredit on an officer as making erroneous reports, and then endeavouring to excuse himself by saying,

"*I must have been mistaken,*" or "*my eyesight must certainly have deceived me.*"

In cases of this importance, everything should be examined with the most perfect attention; he must endeavour to attain an accurate distinction of objects, be provided with an excellent spy-glass, never trust to appearances, and above all, not suffer himself to be imposed, upon through fear. He has it in his power to communicate his observations to old confidential soldiers, and hear their opinion, by which means he will be convinced of the reality of things, and not in danger of mistaking a hundred horse for a whole regiment, or a flock of sheep for a body of infantry.

When an officer is about to make a patrol to some distance, which will require three, four, or more days' absence, he should take with him the *countersign* for as many days as he may think necessary: he should also be provided with one day's forage for his horses, and see that his people be supplied with bread and other necessaries, that they may not be obliged to go into the villages and ask for such articles, a practice which should never take place but by night, and then without making themselves known.

If it can be avoided, he should take no *guide*, but be able to direct his march from the information gained from his map, even though he be an entire stranger to the country: he must avoid also as much as possible all conversation with the inhabitants, especially in an enemy's country, and not suffer his people to form any sort of connection with them, for he certainly will be betrayed if the object of his mission be once discovered. He should select, as much as possible, those of his people who speak the language of the country, that he may the more easily pass as a friend, learn whatever is necessary, and keep himself unknown.

If, during his march, he should be obliged to go near the enemy, he must lie hid by day in some thick wood, and use no fire. Both the horses and men should take this opportunity to rest, and a few dismounted men should be posted as guards in the thickest part of the wood towards the enemy. If the flat country can be discovered from the top of a high tree, a man should be sent thither, but the people who are on this duty are not to fire if they see the enemy, but give the alarm by whistling, or striking their hands upon something, so that if the enemy be advancing in a direct line on the detachment, it may be able to withdraw in silence.

All persons who may come near the place where the detachment lies concealed, such as woodmen, shepherds, or women, should be secured and confined near the detachment till night. The officer is not to ask them any particular question, using only common conversation about the different roads, to keep them ignorant of that which he is about to pursue: in other respects, he should treat them very civilly, and suffer them to depart when he wishes to begin his march. As soon as they are at a sufficient distance to prevent their seeing anything he is to continue his route.

ARTICLE 3

Of Night Patrols

When a commissioned or non-commissioned officer is sent by night with a small party to reconnoitre if the enemy be actually arrived at such a place, and in what force, or indeed on any expedition whatever, he is to form his advanced guard according to the strength of his detachment: this guard should never be far from the main body of the party, but march in such a way as to keep it always in sight, and let *its* movements be a guide for *their* own. The men who march in front and on the flanks will hear any sort of noise, such as the barking of dogs or trampling of horses, much sooner than those who compose the body of the troop, on account of the noise made by the feet of their own horses. The whole detachment should halt every now and then to listen, and frequently dismount to apply their ears to the ground, as by this means footsteps are heard at a great distance.

If dogs frequently bark, it may naturally be supposed that there are some people not far off: in this case, the officer commanding the detachment must endeavour to steal forward to the spot from whence the sound proceeds, with some of the most intelligent of his people, and try to discover, with great caution and silence, what there is going forward.

If the sound proceed from a village where nothing is to be discovered, he should go on dexterously to the first house where he sees a light, and leave his horse in charge of one of his comrades, whilst he creeps along by the hedges, passes through gardens, and inner yards, (sometimes even on all fours if necessary) till he arrives at the window where he saw the light, and then examine if any soldiers of the enemy be there, by knocking gently at the window, and calling out the master of the house. From him he must enquire, in a polite manner, what troops there be in the village, of what force, and if there be any others in the neighbourhood, and then retire quietly to report to the officer commanding the detachment.

If he perceive a fire in any part, he must approach it quietly, (giving his horse in charge, if obliged to go on foot), to learn if they are enemy's troops, and observe as particularly as possible their number and description. But if it prove to be nothing more than a party of shepherds or countrymen, he may learn from them all he wishes to know.

In a strange country, the detachment should always be provided with a guide, and unless satisfied of his fidelity, he should be kept constantly in sight, and tied to one of the party. He may also every now and then be threatened to have his *brains* blown out if he *dare* to conduct the detachment into the hands of the enemy.

As long as the night patrol remains in an open smooth country, small patrols on the flanks (as has been already mentioned) may constantly be sent out. But when it has to pass through a forest, these small patrols should fall back on the main body, particularly if the wood be thick, or the night very dark.—If the wood be not very thick, they may, however, be continued, taking care never to lose sight of the detachment, for fear of going astray and losing themselves.

The officer should order two men on whom he can depend, to march in front at a certain distance, and halt his party often to listen for whistlings or any other signals that have been agreed on between them, that the party may not fall into the hands of the enemy.

When, in a dark night, an officer is to form the advanced guard of a larger detachment, he should order some of his people to go before, and some to follow the party, one by one, so as to form a sort of chain from the advanced guard to the main body, and at every crossing he should leave a man to point out the road which the others have taken.

The greatest attention must be paid to keeping the people awake by night, for if a few in the front should fall asleep and stop suddenly, the people in the rear, being ignorant of the real cause, will halt also, and produce very probably the most disagreeable consequences.

It should be an established rule in all patrols, particularly by night, to select those soldiers who can speak fluently the language of the country, especially if it be that of an enemy, that they may easily pass as friends, and gain from the inhabitants all the information that is required.

The greatest silence must also be observed in the march of patrols by night: no *dogs* or *white* horses should be allowed, nor the horses be subject to neighing: neither must the men be suffered to *speak, strike fire,* or *smoke,* as all these circumstances not only prevent their own hearing, but also serve as information to the enemy on their approach.

If an officer wish particularly to know the hour, he must examine the dial by a piece of lighted *armadou* under his cloak, and the moment he is informed the *armadou* must be extinguished.

The cloaks also which the men wear at night, should not be of a bright colour, as the white or yellow shoulder belts render than sufficiently distinguishable.

When a patrol has to pass bridges or defiles in the night, it's first object should be to visit carefully the environs on each side, and not to proceed till perfectly convinced that no party of the enemy be in the neighbourhood.

If it be the intention to return the same way, one or two men should be left, who are to give intelligence by discharge of pistol if the enemy be near, that the party may take a different route.

If a night expedition of this kind be to take place near, or in front of the enemy's posts, the tanks on the side of the enemy must be opened by small bodies of four or six men belonging to the party, so that if any detachment of the enemy should approach, the march of the main body may not so easily be interrupted: these small bodies may always keep the enemy in check for some little time.

If the detachment should be partly composed of infantry or *chasseurs*, it becomes their duty, particularly in woods, to cover the march of the cavalry.

When a detachment wants forage by night, a few of the men who understand the language of the country should be sent into a village to enquire for it, and bring it to the detachment on their horses, studiously avoiding every kind of outrage or excess to keep the inhabitants ignorant of their strength of the whole party, as well as of their station. Civil behaviour will often prevent their informing the enemy that you have been there.

When a patrol by night shall perceive, without being observed, the approach of an enemy, it should endeavour to ascertain their force, which may be done with tolerable exactness by attending to the *tread* of their *horses*. This intelligence must be immediately conveyed by trusty soldiers to the camp, headquarters, and advanced posts, to put them on their guard. The patrol is then to retire very quietly, and if convinced that the enemy marches with its camp or headquarters, the general commanding should immediately be informed of it: but if the patrol itself be discovered, after a few pistol shots, it should rejoin the grand guard, and endeavour with it to restrain the enemy as long as possible, that the troops of the camp or quarter may be prepared to receive them.

It often happens, that the frequent and sudden appearance of the enemy are only intended to alarm and fatigue our posts: it therefore sometimes becomes necessary to inform the camp or headquarter of such circumstances, without firing or any kind of noise; by this means the enemy are defeated in their intent, and by misconceiving that they take.us by surprise, they themselves are routed and beaten. Another material advantage is, that by avoiding firing, noise, and hurry, all orders that are issued are more regularly executed. Men who are soundly asleep in camp or quarters, on being suddenly awoke, and not aware of the cause, often take to their heels, every one upon his own account, instead of repairing to the places appointed for the squadrons in case of alarm.

But it is often the case, that the enemy does not come slowly on, but on full gallop, in order to mix themselves with the patrols and grand guards, and by that means reach the quarter. Under these circumstances information cannot be too quickly conveyed; it therefore becomes necessary to fire a good deal, and not fall back immediately on the camp or quarter, but take a different direction. Thus the enemy will be pursuing in the dark, going from the camp instead of approaching it, occasioning, it may be, some fortunate circumstance in our favour. But to accomplish this, it is very essential, that the people who are advanced, should be beforehand well instructed, that they may be quite prepared when such circumstances arrive.

When the approach of the enemy is early and silently discovered the great advantage accrues of mounting the people and posting them where the enemy is expected to pass: to entice them still more effectually, the advanced guards may be allotted to remain, and be ordered to post themselves on that side where you are placed. When these retire, they are to keep up a constant firing, and then near the spot where the main party is placed, pass it rapidly: the enemy will of course wish to enter the village with them, expecting support from those without, and as soon as entered, will disperse themselves for the sake of plunder: it is then that the officer who is advantageously posted can fall on the enemy who are without the village, and, though he be inferior in numbers, attack them to advantage, and acquire great reputation.

The grand guard, which hitherto had been drawing on the enemy now returns and falls on those dispersed in: the village, who are unable to resist, and seek their safety in flight. If they find that their companions are beaten, they are very easily made prisoners; but if it be evident that the enemy is so very superior in number, that no advantage can arise from the attack, the troop which was ready to engage must silently retire, inclining to one side.

If an officer commanding a patrol by night has with him some infantry or *chasseurs*, he should order them to compose his flank patrols but when he comes to a forest, he must only suffer two men to march in front, followed by the infantry, divided into two or more parties, according to his force, which are again to be followed by the cavalry, who should also have a rear guard of two men: the flank patrols are to be furnished by the infantry the whole extent of the detachment, as they can pass more easily along the narrow paths, or between the bushes, than the cavalry. As soon as the enemy are perceived, or any firing be heard in front, the infantry must disperse to right and left, out of the road, marching along on each side at certain distances, to the end that whilst the enemy are falling on the two men in front, the course may be clear for them to fall back on the main body, and put themselves in good order to receive the enemy and put them to the route.

When the firing of the infantry has obliged the enemy to retire, great success will frequently attend the pursuit of the cavalry; but if the cavalry should happen to be repulsed, they must fall back through the infantry, who are to support them in their turn. If the whole detachment be obliged to give way, the rear guard is to be furnished by the infantry in the woods, and the cavalry in the open country.

If the officer commanding find that he is pursued by a large body of cavalry, he must divide his infantry into three parties, and his cavalry into two, making only one front of his detachment, so that the cavalry may be in the centre and the infantry on the wings. He may also place here and there a good infantry marksman in the rear of the cavalry: in this manner a good retreat may always be conducted, by making one part rapport the other. The infantry will keep up a constant fire as they retreat, and being supported by the cavalry, will be less exposed than them. The flanks are to be covered by the infantry, and the enemy's cavalry, though superior in number, will not expose itself so readily to fire as the infantry.

But if, on the other hand, each corps be individually put in motion, it often happens that the one abandons the other, and that party which ought singly to have sustained the attack, chooses rather to retire under cover of the night.

If it be impossible to hold out any length of time, some trusty soldiers should be sent to the camp or quarter for reinforcement, to avoid the risk of losing the whole party.

ARTICLE 4
On the Conduct of an Officer on an advanced Post.

When an officer is ordered to go on the wing of an enemy's post or army with thirty or forty cavalry, in order to observe its motions, or cover some part of the country, he should endeavour, by means of maps or more particular information, to gain a perfect knowledge of it. In the first place, he ought to know how to choose his post, which should be as much as possible on a height covered with trees, from whence he can discover all the motions of the enemy, without allowing himself to be perceived.

The post being well chosen, he is to repair to it by night in the greatest silence possible, (particularly if the country be hostile), avoiding all the villages, and every other means of discovering himself: when arrived, the kindling of fire and every kind of noise is strictly to be forbidden. At daybreak he should place some dismounted men on the slope of the hill towards the enemy, behind trees or bushes, who may be able to discover all that is in their front. If sufficient information cannot be attained by this means, people must be placed on the tops of high trees to observe everything with attention, and the officer is to be acquainted, in the most exact circumstantial manner, with all that they can discover.

He is also to observe in person all the enemy's motions, note them in his tablets, and mark the hour, and even the moment, when each particular circumstance happened, so that he may be enabled to render an exact account to the general commanding every evening.

As the chief design of a detachment is to discover others whilst it keeps itself concealed, it is essential that both men and horses should be provided with provisions and forage for three days: at the expiration of this time, it .is generally relieved, but the officer who understands his duty will rather wish to remain on his post.

The new detachment is to be conducted by night with all the foregoing cautions by a man belonging to the old detachment, who knows where to find the officer who brings it: by this means he may remain making his observations a long time before he is discovered. But as soon as he finds, himself perceived by any means, his attention and vigilance must be redoubled: by day he must strive to maintain his post to the best of his power, but as soon as it becomes dark, he should choose some other place in the neighbourhood to pass his nights. From this place (of which no person should be informed beforehand) he will constantly send forward small patrols to secure himself both on the right and left.

Before daybreak he should quit his nocturnal situation, to prevent discovery, and secure for some nights to come quiet and peaceable possession. By day he must ascend some neighbouring height from whence he can discover the enemy: through this means he will always be able to maintain his ground, being the only person informed where he shall pass the following day and night. The night post may be changed, now here and now there, as often as he deems necessary. His choice, however, must always be so made as to enable him to attain the object of his mission. He should have no fixed post, nor should any person have an idea of his designs. The detachment should only be informed of the rallying point at camp, or some other place, in case he should be obliged to disperse them.

No fire should, on any account, be permitted during the night, but in case that anything is absolutely wanted, it should be sought for in the villages that are in the rear: even this, however, is to be avoided if possible.

On the whole, an officer entrusted with so hazardous a commission, must do all in his power to get acquainted with the neighbourhood, its defiles, it's copses, and it's heights, that he may be enabled frequently to change his position. He is, however, always to keep himself concealed, that neither the enemy or the inhabitants may be absolutely certain of his situation. By this means the enemy, if they have any design upon him, must first find him out, which attempt will discover their intentions.

On these occasions, the horses should never be unsaddled, or at farthest not more than one half at a time, should such indulgence prove absolutely necessary. With regard to the men, the officer's personal example and kind treatment will keep their spirits up by day, and their eyes open by night.

As the chief design of an officer commanding a detachment of this nature is to observe the enemy, and reconnoitre a country with which he is acquainted, he ought by no means to busy himself with prisoners or plunder, but execute with judgment the task which has been assigned him, without being discovered or obliged to abandon his post, and having the mortification to see his design miscarry. He ought (if the phrase may be allowed) to be constantly creeping round about the enemy, be very shy of entering any houses by day, and especially of putting the inhabitants to any expense, for in such case they will spare no pains and neglect no means to discover his lurking place, unkennel him, and drive him out of the neighbourhood.

An officer with such a charge has to encounter, most undoubtedly, much of danger and fatigue: but on the other hand, his success will be eminently glorious, for he has to cover an extent of country with a handful of people, which would naturally require a much greater number, especially if the party have less activity than light troops: by this means, therein fore, he performs a very essential service to the army.

As to what remains, he is to put in practice (if he well knew how to apply them) all the rules laid down for the conduct of patrols and of advanced guards.

ARTICLE 5
On the Conduct of an Officer who is sent out to make Prisoners.

This business is to be executed in a variety of ways, depending on the officer's particular idea, local situation, its being day or night, &c. &c. The task itself is not very arduous, but often of great service and utility to the general commanding, when he is unable by spies or other means to gain intelligence of the enemy.

The approach to the enemy is to be conducted in the manner already laid down for the patrols by day. In order to keep concealed, all the villages and high roads are to be avoided, and he must, steal; across the defiles and villages, from copse to copse and height to height, keeping a sharp lookout on every road that the enemy may take.

If he wish to make any discovery from a height, he must ascend it alone, and on foot, leaving his horse at the bottom of the ascent: if the height be entirely void of shelter, he must not wear his hat or any kind of clothings that will make him distinguishable at a distance. He should also alter his appearance, when on the height, to that of a husbandman for instance: in a word, he should have nothing about him that looks soldier-like, as a man who sees at a good distance will easily distinguish a military man from a rustic.

In this manner he must examine very minutely on all sides, and if he discover a party of the enemy of nearly his own force, fall on them with fury, and take some of them prisoners.

During their first surprise, he will ask the most material questions, promising them their liberty if they speak truth, and threatening them with death if they refuse: he is not, however, to place implicit confidence in all they say, but be able to distinguish the possible and the likely from the untrue, to avoid doings himself an injury by making a false report. In an expedition of this nature, an officer must not allow his patience to be exhausted by waiting, lest by being too precipitate, he fall into the snare which he had designed for others.

If he be posted in a copse, and see many people coming towards him from the enemy's country, a man should be sent softly forward in a round-about way, (to conceal from whence he came,) who in some thick part of the copse should put the necessary questions to them; for if he went on strait forward, and a party of the enemy happen to be in the neighbour-hood, the detachment would run the risk of being discovered.

In general, it is necessary on these occasions to make use of many little stratagems, which must depend entirely on the ingenuity of the officer.

When it is dark, the rules laid down for the night patrols are to be observed: the officer must keep a sharp look-out on the enemy's advanced guards, to see if it be not possible to carry off a patrol, and if that does not succeed, take advantage of the night to approach them as near as possible, fall on them with the greatest activity, and carry off all that he can lay hold of.

If any of the officer's party speak the language of the country, he may suffer them to go in front, close to the vedettes, where, by call-ing themselves deserters, and speaking to them on indifferent subjects, they may often approach very near to their posts.

When an officer goes on an expedition of this kind, he should always have with him people on whom he can depend; and that nei-ther he nor they may lose their money, and had better be cautioned beforehand, and have it lodged in the regimental chest, or some safe hands, taking a proper security for it: for it will sometimes happen that a man, who on other occasions is very brave, will neglect to execute his duty where there is a chance of losing his property.

If the detachment want provisions or forage, they are to be pro-cured by night, in the manner already mentioned.

ARTICLE 6

Of the Manner in which an Officer should attack a Body of the Enemy's heavy Cavalry

In case that an officer is detached with thirty, forty, or fifty men, as a patrol, or with any other view, and he meets with a party of *cuiras-siers* or heavy dragoons belonging to the enemy, he should endeavour, as much as possible; to conceal the strength of his own party, not discovering more than are barely necessary to observe the force and appearance of the enemy.

If he know how to profit of this advantage, he will be enabled to make a stand against them, though they exceed his numbers by more than half. He ought to examine if they have marched any distance, if the horses be tired, and their baggage with them, if the road by which they came be bad or otherwise, if the country be swampy, if the horses sink or the soil be firm, if they march on a plain or in a defile, and whether possible to surround them. He should be master of all these circumstances at one view, concealing himself at a distance, or shewing but a small part of his force. His future arrangements must depend entirely on circumstances.

If he perceive that he cannot attack them to advantage on their march, he must suffer them to pass quietly on, keeping at a certain distance with a few of his people, (the major part being concealed), as if disinclined or afraid to attack them, till they arrive at a situation more favourable to his design. He is then to divide his detachment into four, five, or six parties, and begin the attack on the weakest side, of which an intelligent officer ought always to be a judge.

A very little time will convince him of the capacity of the officer opposed to him, and the good or bad order of his people, from whence he will easily conclude if any advantage be to be gained.

It should ever be an officer's design to fatigue and harass the enemy's horse, by drawing them on to soft ground where the heavy cavalry readily sink, and obliging them to a variety of manoeuvres, with a view of throwing them into disorder. If he carry this point, his success is certain,

The attack is then to be made on all sides, and when every fear of resistance be done away, he may give quarter: if it be necessary, however, the horses may be killed till he finds himself completely master of the enemy, and that they are flying: at this period he may be allowed to take some prisoners.

All that can be done by the officers of the enemy in such situation is, either to send a part of their people towards us, or wait steadily and without moving to receive us. In the first case, they must be attacked and beat back to the body of the party as soon as possible, our troops mixing with them: during this period, the other parties are to make a general attack on all sides, occasioning universal disorder. In the second case, we should endeavour to surround them on all sides, keeping up a general fire; and as they will be obliged to turn against those who take them in the rear, that favourable moment should be employed in charging them to advantage.

But if the enemy's officer be a man of experience, the moment he sees any people coming towards him, he will take such a position as to secure his rear, and only subject himself to be attacked in front. It will then be very difficult, if not impossible, to make anything of him. In this case, the wisest part to take is, to withdraw to a certain distance, and suffer the enemy to continue their march, but to follow sufficiently close to take advantage of any favourable position to employ the means already laid down.

ARTICLE 7

On the Conduct of an Officer towards a Party of Hussars of equal Strength with his own

When an officer falls in with a detachment of hussars of equal strength with his own, fortune generally decides in favour of the best men and the best horses, who attack their adversary vigorously, though they should be fired on, and never suffer themselves to give way, but fall resolutely on them without making any use of their firearms.

There are, however, many advantages to be derived from being in an open country, which will more happily forward this design.

Supposing his detachment to consist of forty men, the first line should be composed of twenty-five, and the second of fifteen, to shew a larger front to the enemy, but this arrangement must take place without the adversary's knowledge: the rear rank is then to be so disposed, that the flank files of the front rank be always covered, to give the appearance of the ranks being complete; the enemy, conceiving of course that the detachment is stronger than it really is, will be the more afraid to attack it. In this order we may march directly towards them, and when the horses are on a full trot, oblique a little, I will suppose towards the right, to take the enemy on the left wing, and if they have not paid immediate attention to this manoeuvre, they will be easily outflanked on the left and beaten.

But if the enemy perceive the intention, they will naturally make a movement to the left, to avoid being flanked: as soon as we find this, five or six men filing from our left (who have been well instructed how to proceed) should fall on the enemy's right wing, whilst the rest attack the left, sword in hand. By this means you endeavour to throw them into disorder and confusion, which will occasion their defeat.

ARTICLE 8

On the Conduct of an Officer in an Affair of Consequence.

An officer who is commanded with a body of men to cover an army or regiment whilst they are deploying, (many are often employed on this service,) should have his eye as well towards the enemy as towards the army which he is designed to cover. He must send out flankers towards the enemy, who, by keeping up a constant firing, will endeavour to disperse them: in this interval he is to pay attention to the movements in his rear, so that he may be always near his own party, and be able to take up the same position that is adopted by the larger body. As soon as he hears a retreat or march sounded, he should collect his people as expeditiously as possible, and fall into the interval allotted for him.

If he be to cover another body of cavalry besides his own, and to which he does not belong, he must betake himself to the nearest wing, join in the attack, and cover the flank, if the enemy wish to make an impression there. If he succeed in breaking the enemy, he must endeavour, if possible, to put them entirely to the route.

As soon as the enemy attempt to rally, he must strenuously exert himself to prevent them, taking care that he is properly supported, and not run the risk, by advancing too far, of being surrounded.

ARTICLE 9

How an Officer ought to cover a Second Line.

Supposing that the first line has six squadrons to cover it, and the second line only four, these last must nevertheless be placed directly behind the right wing of the first line. With these four squadrons the officer commanding is to check the enemy, should they be disposed to make an impression on the flank of the second line. If he perceive that the enemy makes an impression on the flanks during the attack, he must hasten to their support, and attack the enemy's flank himself, taking care in doing this, that he does not expose the flank of the second line, and abandon it to the enemy.

If the first line has broken the enemy, and is mixed with it, the second line will naturally come up to its support; but if the second line be composed of heavy cavalry that cannot move quickly enough, the officer with the party must still follow the first line, keeping himself compact, in order to receive prisoners. What follows, regards the officers of each wing of the second line.

Article 10

On the Conduct of an Officer on an advanced Post, when the main Body of the Army is in Cantonments.

The welfare and safety of an entire army often depends on a detachment of this nature. An officer, therefore, who is appointed to such a command, cannot use too much circumspection for the safety of the army behind him. I will imagine his force to consist entirely of light cavalry.

Supposing, then, that an officer has thirty or forty men given to him, with which he is to occupy a certain village; as soon as he arrives he must make a patrol of a third or fourth part of his force, and push it as far as he can with safety to the right and left, even to the enemy's posts. He should reconnoitre all the villages, copses, and defiles that are in his front, placing the remainder of his detachment, during this examination, under cover behind the village, but if he fear an attack, they should all accompany him.

When the patrol is finished, he must take with him a man of the village on horseback, to shew him all the particular objects in the neighbourhood of his post, on which side the enemy is situate, and by what roads or defiles they can approach him, having recourse at the same time to his chart, in order to gain a more perfect knowledge of the country.

As soon as this business is completed, he must place his vedettes in such a way, that they can see the whole extent of the country towards the enemy, as has been already said with respect to the advanced guards: a few of his people should also be sent to the top of the village steeple with some of the peasants who are well acquainted with the surrounding conn. try, to observe attentively all that passes, and when they discover the enemy, give the signal by one stroke on the bell: if there be no village steeple, he must send one man to the top of the highest house.

When an officer has made his patrol agreeably to the rules laid down, he may allow half of his party to go into the nearest peasants' houses, unsaddle, unbridle, and feed half of the horses, and when they have finished, suffer the remaining half to do the same. But if the enemy be in the neighbourhood, and an attack to be feared, he must remain hid in the rear of the village, and feed his horses tied to a hedge.

It is also necessary to have a guard on foot, who can always see the vedettes, and who are to report the least movement that they may make. Nor is it of less importance that posts should be placed on both sides of the village, especially if the country be hilly or abounding in copses, to cover the flanks, and prevent attack or surprise from those quarters.

In a word, security is to be regarded as the first object, not only in front, but also on the flanks and in the rear, particularly at night, even though we are convinced that we have friends posted in our neighbourhood.

The officer should frequently send small patrols of two or three men in front of the vedettes, who are to endeavour to gain heights which are at too great a distance for established posts, and try to discover something relative to the enemy.

He may also make patrols of this kind in person, with fifteen, twenty, and even thirty men, to shew himself to the enemy, and by that means make them believe that he is stronger than he really is. By doing this, the advantage will accrue of knowing more intimately the distance and position of the enemy.

By day, half the horses may be unsaddled, and half the people allowed to sleep, the other half remaining saddled and bridled. At nightfall, the patrols should be made in the neighbourhood and in front of the vedettes, (the officer himself being present), to discover if any change has taken place. He is then to report, in writing if possible, to the general.

When night is quite come on, the vedettes should fall back, and if they were placed on heights, they should now descend to the low ground, as by night it is much more easy to discover a person when looking upwards, than if you have to look into a bottom.

If there be a forest or any defiles leading to the village, which the vedettes can see only by day, posts should be placed in them: if any bridges be in front, the vedettes should remain there by day, and fall back at night, taking care that the bridges be stripped.

All the wide and public entrances to the village should be *barricadoed* with carriages, trees, or bars, and peasants placed there as guards, who should, nevertheless, be frequently visited, lest of themselves they open the passage.

The officer should inform his people who are without the village, of two or three secret avenues which are unknown to the enemy: with these passages the men must make themselves perfectly acquainted, that they may be able to find them readily by night, or in case of necessity. It is by these passages, (known only to the detachment), that

131

the officer will send out by night small patrols to visit the vedettes, and go along the whole extent of the chain. About midnight the officer will do well to be particularly attentive to his guards, and if the enemy attempt anything, conduct himself according to the plan laid down for night patrols. Towards morning, even before daybreak, the whole detachment must mount, and if the officer has thought proper to shift his ground during the night, the night posts are to be informed of it, that they may know where to find him. A report is then to be made immediately to the general commanding, or to the officer who sent out the detachment, of all that has passed during the night, particularly if the enemy has made any movement, or has discovered his approach; in this case the officer's vigilance should be redoubled: he should be constantly in the open country, and conduct himself in every respect as has been directed under the article of. advanced guards.

As soon as the day begins to dawn, the vedettes must gradually resume their posts, keeping a sharp lookout on all sides: small patrols should also be kept ready to move forward and scour the copses and neighbouring country. If no party of the enemy have crept thither, these men may remain there till broad day: this precaution is particularly necessary in cloudy weather, and they may disperse themselves and cover the whole front. If all be quiet, the officer himself should advance, and endeavour to make some discovery; in which case the patrols should file away in front, as far as he shall deem practicable. During this period the whole detachment should be mounted and ready on any emergency.

When all the patrols are returned, the officer should report to the general whatever he has learnt relating to the enemy, and then send a man again to the top of the steeple or highest house, unsaddle and feed half his horses, and endeavour to prevent any inhabitant of the country from going towards the enemy, to betray him or discover his position.

It would not be amiss to acquaint all the inhabitants of the neighbourhood also, that if any of them go in front of the posts towards the enemy, the vedettes are ordered to kill them immediately. But if an occasion should offer for sending forwards a trusty man, it should certainly be done, though it cost a little money, as more intelligence is to be gained by these means than by the patrols, measures can be taken more advantageously, and a more exact and particular report made, which should be done, if possible, morning and evening.

For what remains to be undertaken in this situation, all the means laid down for advanced guards, day and night patrols, and reconnoi-trings, (made use of as fundamental principles,) may be employed.

On the Duty of an Officer detached with twenty, thirty, or forty Horse, to occupy a Village in Front, or on the Flank of an Army whilst it is in Winter Quarters.

It is to be presumed, that when an officer is commanded to take possession of a situation with which he is acquainted, that the general has given him all the necessary instructions; such as, on what side he is particularly to have his eye, what part he is to cover particularly more than others, whither be should send his patrols, to what posts of the enemy he is to pay particular attention, and on what side to retreat, if attacked by superior force.

An officer in this situation is supposed to remain some time on his post, being generally relieved every two days or twenty-four hours, according as the duty of the post may be fatiguing, or require much attention.

Two cases may here be supposed,—the detachment consisting en-tirely of cavalry, or of cavalry and infantry.

The dispositions to be made in these cases are exactly similar to those already laid down: but as both the climate and roads are ma-terially changed in winter, the officer will do well to attend to the following cautions:—

When arrived at his post and he has patroled to reconnoitre the neighbourhood, he should take with him a man of the village as a guide, and amongst other questions inquire of him, if the sides of the road are passable after a fall of snow: he will also carefully observe all the country round, that he may take his measures accordingly, cov-er the parts most exposed, choose the fittest places for his advanced guards and vedettes, and appoint an alarm post for the detachment in case of an alert. Hereafter he will receive more particular instructions.

As neither men nor horses can keep the open field in this season as in summer, that side of the village should be chosen which is the least exposed. The people should occupy houses, whose back doors open on the place of *rendezvous*, and the officer should take care that they be not too much dispersed: a non-commissioned officer should also remain in each house, to have an eye on the rest, and particularly to keep them awake by night. The officer's quarter should be chosen as near the centre of his party as possible, with a sentinel on foot to give an alarm on the first discharge of a pistol. If it be necessary, all the people may assemble by night in the officer's quarter, that he may be guarded against every accident. He must not allow carriages, pieces of timber, or other obstacles to remain in the streets of the village, that may incommode his people, if they should be obliged to be on horseback by night.

An officer should never indulge himself in the idea of his being on a secure post, that he has a superior force, or that the enemy is too far distant to come on him quickly, as nothing is more deceiving or dangerous. We have but too many instances where this misplaced security has been the cause of surprise, and where the watchful and diligent man has been more than a match for the sleepy and slothful. To avoid surprise, we should ever be as watchful as if close to an enemy constantly disponed to attack us.

There is no necessity for attending to a soldier's grumblings, who is naturally never satisfied; on the contrary, he should be convinced, that the situation which he occupies requires all such cautions, as the least negligence might prove of material advantage to the enemy. If, notwithstanding all these attentions, any misfortune should happen, (which will seldom be the case), the satisfaction will remain of having exerted our utmost endeavours to do our duty.

All that can be undertaken or done on a post of this nature, is with a view to gain time, that the detachment be not attacked unawares, but be always under arms at the place of assembly, and in a situation to resist the enemy, or inform the army of their approach.

The patrols should be well instructed how to march, and on which side, never going out at regular hours, for fear of being observed, and carried off by the enemy.

If any enterprise on the part of the enemy be to be feared, the whole detachment should be collected together (no matter at what hour) on the alarm post, or at the officer's quarter, and wait for daybreak in that situation.

In general, the people should be kept awake, during the whole night, even in their quarters, and for this the non-commissioned officers are to be held responsible.

The officer himself must frequently visit his posts during the night, and shew himself in the village, for the people, knowing their chief to be on the watch, will be more alert themselves: he may also take a man with him, now from this house and now from that, to attend him whilst visiting his posts. When the detachment finds that the officer does not spare himself, they will give him their esteem and confidence, and follow him anywhere, and at any hour.

A sentinel on foot should always be placed at the officer's door, and if a trumpeter be with the detachment, he also should be quartered near him.

If the enemy approach the posts by day, the officer must instantly mount his detachment, and hasten to the support of his advanced guards, or to allow them to fall back on him, if necessary. If it happen by night, he will immediately dispatch some men in front of the enemy to those entrances of the village which are only known to the advanced guards, to support them, and allow them to fall back.

Every practicable means must be employed to attain this end, as the safety of the whole army is concerned. For this reason, he must try to check the enemy, though superior in number, and endeavour to draw them away from the quarter. Immediate report should be made of what passes to the general commanding, that a reinforcement may arrive, and the detachment be enabled to fall back on the body of the army.

Further, all the methods before mentioned for the safety of quarters, advanced guards, patrols, and reconnoitrings, may also here be employed.

In dark, stormy weather, the vedettes should not only be brought nearer each other at equal distances, but they should also visit each other alternately, so that no space be left uncovered, by which through favour of the night an enemy might, pass.

If infantry should compose a part of the detachment, they ought to be placed in houses fronting the enemy, that they may be ready on the first signal to throw themselves along the hedges and entrances of the village, and support the people that are posted without. All the large avenues of the village which are barred by carriages and pieces of timber, should also be lined with infantry. By day, these guards may keep themselves on some heights beyond the barriers, from whence they can behold the vedettes, but at night they must retire within them.

Posts of infantry should also be placed at those particular entries to which attention has been paid, and if the cavalry should be obliged to make use of them, the sentries are to close them again the moment that they are passed, to prevent the enemy from penetrating the village. This body of infantry should endeavour to keep the enemy in check as long as possible, and when returning towards the rallying point, should pass across the courts and gardens, when by meeting the cavalry and mutually supporting each other, they will often succeed in repulsing the enemy.

It is very essential, that an officer commanding a post of this nature, should endeavour to promote a good understanding between the cavalry and infantry, taking particular care that the latter are well put up, for as they are not much accustomed to a life of ease, they will do all in their power to defend and keep possession of good quarters.

For whatever more may be required in these circumstances, regard must be had to what has been already said under the article of spies.

ARTICLE 12.
On the Manner in which an Officer Commanding a Party of Cavalry, should attack a Quarter that is occupied by Hussars

If an officer wish to signalise himself by engaging in an affair with an enemy of superior force, he should propose to himself an attack on a quarter that is occupied by hussars, as being the most agreeable, easy, and certain way of acquiring reputation.

But to insure success in this enterprise, he must begin by procuring the most exact information of all the particulars of the village and neighbourhood which the enemy possess. He should know for a certainty what officer commands the post, if he be experienced and well informed, or young, ignorant, and wedded to self-opinion. For an officer of the latter description always fancies himself sufficiently secure where he has posted his vedettes, occupied the avenues leading to the village by a *sorry* guard, and sent out patrols at *certain* hours, and on *well-known* roads.

He ought also to know if his adversary trust to the superiority of his troop, for in that case he generally thinks himself wrong if any of his arrangements betray a fear of the enemy, and from that circumstance often exposes himself from too much caution.

He should likewise be instructed of all the means of defence which the enemy possess in the village, on what side their people are quartered, and where the alarm post is situate: what description of troops they are, if picked men or drafts from different corps: if in case of alarm by night, the people are all assembled in one house, or suffered to be scattered about in their quarters: if any assistance can be sent to them, and from what point, and how much time it would require to arrive at the post attacked. He ought also to know in what manner the advanced guards are placed by night and day, and what are the hours, and what the destinations chosen by the patrols.

When sufficiently informed on all these subjects, he will of course make his disposition for the attack, which could not possibly commence earlier. The affair may take place by night or day; I shall begin with the latter—

If he be convinced that the officer keeps a good look-out by night, and conducts himself in such a manner as entirely to prevent being surprised, he must endeavour to gain his point by day.

The advanced guards of the enemy are not to be disturbed, but we are to pass by them on one side through open roads where there is no wood or hollow way; this undertaking is big with difficulties, if not altogether impracticable, but in a mountainous country, or one that is full of copses, the following method may be observed:—

If the enemy's quarter be far distant, the march should be begun at dark night or in a fog, and continued towards a village, copse, or valley in the neighbourhood, or on one of the flanks of the enemy: to obtain this point, we must avoid falling in with the enemy's patrols, and when arrived, wait patiently the coming day, or until their patrols are returned into their quarters. If we have escaped their sight, and they in consequence have reported that they have met with nothing, their officer will most probably put his people under cover, order them to lay by their arms, feed their horses, and even unsaddle them, for they will conclude themselves to be in safety, and be glad to procure a little sleep, which is denied them by night.

The advanced guard then fall *full gallop* on the enemy's advanced guard, to prevent their mounting, or entering the village with them: enter the village and disperse themselves, firing their pistols through the windows to increase the confusion. The officer's quarter should be pointed out to some daring fellows, who will immediately repair thither, and seize his person, or at least prevent his getting on horseback. If the advanced guard can arrive at the village without engaging the advanced guard of the enemy, so much the better, for when they see that we are possessed of the village, they will not expose themselves by endeavouring to enter, but rather decamp, by which means we shall have fewer enemies to encounter.

The officer, with his troop divided into two parts, should follow pretty closely the advanced guard: one part must support the advanced guard, and cut to pieces everyone who presents himself, without taking prisoners, till the enemy is entirely in their power: the other part should remain without the village, regularly formed: if there be not a second officer, the command must be given to a non-commissioned officer, who should post a few men here and there on the heights, to be able at the same time to observe the approach of a reinforcement, and inform the detachment of it.

The officer himself should visit different parts of the village to give his orders, keep his people together, and prevent pillaging: against this practice he must give particular cautions beforehand, and threaten those that may offend with the most exemplary punishment, explaining to each individual what he has to do.

All prisoners are to be delivered up to the party who remain without the village, to hinder the people from dragging them about here and there, which would prevent their taking others. They should be instructed beforehand, that when they give up their prisoners to the party, they are to give their own names, and those of the people whom they have taken, that after the business is over, every man may know his own prisoners. For want of this precaution, the soldiers often keep their prisoners with them, and the officer finds himself left alone, instead of every man being employed in making as many prisoners as he can.

The trumpeter, if there be any with the detachment, should remain with the party without the village.

The officer must be very attentive to the time he stays on this expedition, lest it fail by the arrival of a reinforcement to the enemy, or himself with his detachment be surprised and made prisoners.

When all the prisoners that can be taken are secured, the officer should order the retreat to be sounded, and the non-commissioned officers to assemble without the village: the prisoners are then to be given in charge to the men who are the *worst* mounted, and put into the shortest road. The officer with the rest of his party will follow at a convenient distance, forming himself, for the sake of security, into a rear guard.

Article 13

On an Attack by Night on a Quarter occupied by Hussars

If, for the reasons laid down in the preceding article, an attack be proposed on a quarter of hussars by night, it should be begun by approaching as near as possible to the village where they are cantoned, avoiding the advanced guards, arriving at the intended point, if possible, from behind by going about, and endeavouring to prevent the enemy from assembling.

In order to attain the first object, the advanced guard with the flankers near to each other must move forward in silence, and endeavour to approach the enemy. As soon as the flankers find they are discovered, they should fall on the enemy *full gallop*, and endeavour to mix with them, without allowing them to mount, or accompany them into the village.

The distribution of his party is first to take place, which cannot properly be done without having some idea of the force of the enemy. Suppose the party *attacked* to be fifty in number, and the *attackers* only twenty-five or thirty, the arrangements are to be made in the following manner:—

A non-commissioned officer with ten men forms the advanced guard, who are already acquainted with the enemy's rallying point, in case of an alert: as soon as he has entered the village with the enemy, he must make directly for this spot, and take possession of it, killing and dispersing whatever comes in his way.

The second party, consisting also of ten, will follow the first pretty closely, enter the village with them, and then disperse to prevent the enemy from rallying, hashing every individual as he presents himself: this is not the moment for making prisoners, but must be delayed till the enemy can no longer resist, or that they have surrendered themselves.

The third party of five will also follow the first, keeping their files close, that they may be in readiness to repair to any spot where the enemy appear to intend resistance, or where the greatest uproar prevails, in order to support the suffering party.

The fourth party, composed also of five, must remain drawn up without the village, to receive the prisoners that are brought to them. But if they perceive that the enemy are beaten, a part of them may also be detached to ramble round the village, and pick up those who wish to escape on foot.

The quarter of the officers, as has been already said, should be the first object of the people appointed to that service, and the officers, if possible, made prisoners. The other men should scatter themselves about the village, to prevent the enemy from mounting, or assembling together.

The officer will most certainly endeavour to escape, by passing through the garden or some other opening, that he may be able to rally his people: but though he should succeed in this, the *third* detachment will be sufficiently strong to disperse them again, and when the officers are once taken, no one will remain to give orders, or get the people together.

The officer who commands should be personally present to give all the necessary orders, and as soon as the affair is finished, he ought to retire in the manner proposed for an attack by day.

In a *night* expedition of this nature, every kind of pillage must be very particularly forbidden, for if this be suffered, the soldier neglects his chief object, and thinks he can in security commit such baseness as tarnishes the most noble exploit, forfeits the reputation of an officer, makes the whole enterprise miscarry, and leads the detachment into the very snare which they had prepared for the enemy.

The retreat is to be conducted in the same manner as proposed in the attack by day.

In night expeditions it is also necessary to make use of some mark or signal to know each other, such as, the turning of the pelisses, wearing the cloaks, or putting a piece of white linen on one arm, a green bough in the cap, or choosing some particular word, which must be given to the people beforehand, that they may know each other in the dark: for want of this caution, very serious inconvenience often happens.

ARTICLE 14

On the Conduct of an Officer who is ordered to put a Country under Contribution

It is to be supposed, that when an officer is sent to put a country under contribution, or to procure provisions for the army, that the country is quite free of the enemy.

Under these circumstances, the general will give him all the orders and means that are necessary to the execution of his commission, as it is seldom left to an officer to receive on his own account the contributions of a whole country. He is in general only charged to make good the requisites to the general, by means of hostages, threats, or even force. So that as long as the country in question refuse not the contribution demanded, it is by no means to be distrained on: and the officer must keep his people in perfect good order, forbidding the least excess, and ordering them to be content with common fare both for themselves and horses. By these means he will the more easily accomplish his end, and the inhabitants will be better able to comply with his demands, than if tormented by too much teasing or pecuniary extortion.

On these occasions, the officer should never suffer his private interest to render him forgetful of the object of his mission, *viz.* the welfare of the whole army. Moreover, he must remain with his detachment till ordered by the general to remove, or till the inhabitants have furnished the necessaries demanded.

Besides this, he ought not to neglect his personal safety, as it is very easy to imagine that he stands in some danger from people who are obliged to *come down* largely. The peasants, whilst they are supposed to be employed in getting their goods together, will use every means to rid themselves of their guests, and inform the nearer enemy of what is going forward, that by their arrival the project may be defeated, and their property preserved. In this case the officer will do well to keep patrols, constantly moving round the villages under contribution, which are situated near the enemy, to gain from them certain intelligence of their appearance, whether they be still or in motion, and if any reinforcements arrive.

According to these circumstances he must regulate his conduct, either hastening the contributions, or allowing more time to the inhabitants, without proceeding to extremities. He should report to the general every motion of change of the enemy, so that if it be their object to prevent the contribution, measures may be taken accordingly, and another detachment sent to his support. Thus situate, he will be able to accomplish his purpose. In a word, every part of his duty must be strictly attended to, and executed with the utmost exactness.

There still remains a case, where an officer may be ordered to levy a contribution on a country which is not absolutely occupied by the enemy, but rendered suspicious by patrols or continual detachments.

This only happens when the country in front is unfavourable for *him*, but convenient for *the enemy* to halt, and pay troublesome visits. For this reason, every means should be used to prevent the enemy from tarrying there, and exerting themselves to rob us of the necessaries of which we stand in need. It is also possible that a party may want provisions, or may have received express orders from the king to raise contributions in a country, for punishment or some other reason. In both these cases, the officer will be obliged, to enable him to gain his point, to make arrangements totally different from those which he would employ, if he had no enemy to fear, or if they were at such a distance as not to disturb him in his expedition.

To insure success, it will therefore be necessary for him to have a perfect knowledge of the country: he should also be informed, if the enemy come thither with whole detachments, or only sent frequent patrols, how they behave to the inhabitants, whether by pillage or any other outrage they render themselves disagreeable. He must also endeavour to make the people his friends, that he may gain intelligence relating to the enemy.

To give some security to his patrols, he should know whither and into what villages the enemy have been most accustomed to send patrols, of what force, what route they take, the moment of their arrival and departure, at what distance the troops are that furnish the patrols; and, in short, whether the country be hilly, swampy, or intersected by small wood, or any other objects. To learn these particulars, he should be furnished with an intelligent spy, and an accurate map of the country.

As expeditions of this nature will not allow an officer to divide his people without great risk, he had better attempt his march in form of patrols, with an advanced and rear guards and flank patrols, endeavouring nevertheless to conceal himself as much as possible. He must consequently instruct his people, that on the least discovery of the enemy, they are to halt and inform him of it, that he may take another road: but if he be so lucky as to gain the village unperceived, he must not go directly into it, but halt in the nearest copses or valleys. From thence, he should detach one or two trusty non-commissioned officers, with six or eight men, into the villages which are not occupied by the enemy, and which are nearer to the army than that where he is posted. In general, it is necessary that the greatest prudence be observed, unless the officer chooses to return empty handed, or run the risk of being carried off.

But in order to gain his point, the officer and non-commissioned officers (who will have received their instructions beforehand) should so place their advanced guards that they may discover everything on the side of the enemy, not neglecting to send forward frequent patrols. They must, however, avoid every village, marching in such a way as to conceal themselves, and still observe everything. The officer should remain with his detachment, without the village which ought to contribute, in a copse or some covered place, shifting his position as often as he shall find necessary, to prevent being found by the enemy, from a deserter, or by any other means. He must, however, never change his post without informing his people who are out where they may find him. The non-commissioned officers commanding the detached posts should all be informed of the place of assembly, in case of being surprised by the enemy.

These precautions being observed, the officer must send some men into the village, who are to bring back with them the magistrate and other chief inhabitants. But to prevent their seeing the strength of his detachment, he should order one party to fall back into the wood, that he may appear in more force them he really is. He must acquaint these inhabitants that they are to deliver, and by what time. They will of course, make all the difficulties and remonstrances possible, in order to gain time and delay the delivery. But as these situations will not allow of much parley, he must explain himself to them very seriously, detain the most wealthy of them, and send the rest back to the village, threatening to set fire to it at the four corners, if the requisition be not delivered by the time appointed.

The advanced guards and patrols must take good care that whilst the contribution is raising, no person goes from the village towards the enemy, and lay hold of every one they meet who wishes to pass.

As soon as the requisition is got together, it is to be loaden on waggons, and sent away by night in charge of a non-commissioned officer and a few men; the officer also will follow by the same route given him for the army, having obtained a certificate from the inhabitants, to produce to the general, and prove that everything has been done for the good of the service. All the non-commissioned officers also, who may be detached in other villages, must in like manner, receiving certificates of what has been delivered, to prevent any excess being committed, either by themselves or their people.

The officer may also take with him some of the inhabitants to attest the good behaviour of the party. When the different deliveries are made, the parties must acquaint each other of their departure, and every part is to be charged with the covering of the waggons that are in front of it, till they all arrive at the army.

ARTICLE 15

On Alarm Posts

By an alarm post we are to understand a certain point where a party is to assemble, in case of alarm, surprise, or approach of an enemy. It is not a matter of indifference how this place is chosen, so as to be in a condition to assemble, and shew a face to the enemy.

When the place is to be fixed on, the village and all its environs are to be well examined, to know if the country be smooth, hilly, or intersected by woods or rivers. Distinction should also be made, whether it would answer the purpose by day or by night, if the ground can contain many different bodies of troops, or only light troops.

If there be any hussars in the village, the alarm post must not be in front towards the enemy, but in the rear, (particularly at night,) and towards that side from whence we can be supported; as otherwise the enemy might prevent our rallying, and disperse the people as fast as they come out of the village.

By day, a spot may be chosen in front of the village, and on that side where the advanced guard is placed, to cover that as well as the quarters.

If the environs are too level, and the enemy can approach the village on every side, the detachment had better assemble in the rear of the village, and be kept awake the whole night. From this spot small patrols should constantly be sent out. The officer or non-commissioned officer of the advanced guard must also be made acquainted with this situation, that in case he has a report to make, or is repulsed by the enemy, he may know where to find the main body of the party.

If the country be much intersected, the alarm post, both by day and night, should be chosen behind some defiles, through which the enemy are obliged to pass, as by this means a small party can defend itself against a much superior force.

It would be an egregious error, to choose an alarm post in front of a defile, at least if it be not covered by a body of infantry.

The moment any alert happens during the night, the detachment must assemble as quickly as possible in the rear of the village, to keep the enemy in check, till the whole of it be got together. If then, on account of superiority, it should be obliged to retire, it should be done very coolly, to allow time for the troops in the rear to put themselves in good order to support you, receive the enemy, and make a glorious affair of it.

The places of rendezvous, both by night and day, should be pointed out to the people by the commanding officer, and the officer ought always to be the *first* on the spot to give their orders, and form the people as they arrive.

ARTICLE 16

On the Military *Coup D'Œil.*

According to the Chevalier Folard's system, the knowledge of the nature and qualities of a country which is the theatre of war, is a science to be acquired. It is the perfection of that art, to learn at one just and determined view, this benefits and disadvantages of a country where posts are to be placed, and how to act to the annoyance of the enemy. This is, in a word, the true meaning of a *coup d'œil,* without which an officer may commit errors of the greatest consequence. In short, without this knowledge, success cannot be promised in any enterprise, as the business of war requires much practice and experience to be well understood. To learn this before we begin a campaign, and, when engaged in it, to be able to join practice to theory, is the business of every good officer.

But as we are not always at war, as the army is not always campaigning, and the regiments only assemble at certain periods for exercise, we must endeavour to improve ourselves by means of our own genius and imagination, so as to learn, even in time of peace, a science so useful and necessary.

In the opinion of the Chevalier Foulards, field diversions are the best calculated to give a military *coup d'œil,* for we not only learn from thence to distinguish the difference of countries, which never resemble each other, but we also get acquainted with a variety of stratagems, all of which have some connection with the business of war. One of the great advantages which we derive from hunting, is the knowledge of different countries, which gives us a *coup d'œil* almost imperceptibly, which a little reflection and practice will soon make perfect.

Besides hunting, by which few people have an opportunity to profit, travels and walks have their advantages.

Whilst travelling, we can look with a penetrating eye over all the country that we pass, figure to ourselves an enemy's post at whatever distance we please, conceive ourselves on another, judge of all the benefits and disadvantages peculiar to each party, arrange in imagination the plan of attack and defence of our own post, and as the unceasing variation of country offers incessantly new discoveries, an imagination a little warmed will never want employment.

Whilst walking, the eye may judge and measure the distance of one place or thing from another; and to be certain that we are not mistaking, we can walk it over and convince ourselves of the justness of our *coup d'œil.*

Every country will furnish an officer, who wishes for instruction, with the means of exercising his eyes and ideas: whilst he who engages in the profession from necessity, without any taste, will let slip the most happy opportunities of improving himself without turning them to any advantage.

www.ingramcontent.com/pod-product-compliance
Lightning Source LLC
Chambersburg PA
CBHW021006090426
42738CB00007B/674